Air Fryer + Keto Air Fryer Cookbook for Busy People

2 Books in one

The Only Book You Need for every model of Air Fryer to Prepare Tasty and Crispy Meals in No Time

Nichole S. Rodriguez

By reading this document, the reader agrees that under no circumstances is the author responsible for any losses, direct or indirect, which are incurred as a result of the use of information contained within this document, including, but not limited to, errors, omissions, or inaccuracies.

TABLE OF CONTENTS

—

INTRODUCTION

The secret of Air Fryer is the unique cooking technology that uses hot-air that circulates inside the fryer. It works no different than any other thermic-processing method, but without all the detrimental side-effects you get when you eat deep-fried foods, for example. You may be able not only to fry but also to bake, broil, roast, rotisserie, and steam things as well. Air Fryer can also be a great substitute for your microwave, oven, or a stove. Except it's much healthier, easier, and faster to use.

On top of that, you can use an air fryer to prepare batters and marinades. The only thing that you should never put in there is generally speaking liquids. That means that things like broth or other soups are not coming at play here. Remember, safety comes first. But given the wide variety of other things you can do with it - it's a tiny con.

Air fryer benefits

Almost no fat and oil involved

Probably the biggest benefit of using the Air Fryer is reducing the amount of oil or other fats you normally use to cook your meals. With the help of Air Fryer as much as one tablespoon is enough to gain the same effect as if you were cooking regular deep fried fries or spring rolls. As hot air circulates inside of the chamber, it makes the food crispy on the outside and tender on the inside.

Fewer calories

Needless to say, as you reduce the amount of fat in your meals, their calorific value drops as well. So not only you eat overall healthier but even your "cheat meals" are less of a problem now. As you can see, using an air fryer can effectively help you drop some extra weight. Maybe it's time you reinstated your relationship with French fries?

It's compact, and it fits everywhere

Because it takes so little space on the kitchen countertop, you don't have to worry about additional clutter. It also doesn't kill the aesthetics of your countertop. You can also put all the accessories inside the fryer, so you reduce unnecessary mess to a 0 level. See how you can start enjoying being in the kitchen again.

How to use an air fryer?

Prepare the air fryer

Some recipes will require using a basket, a rack, or a rotisserie. Some other recipes require cake or muffin pans. Before you pick the recipe and prepare your accessories, make sure they fit into your fryer.

Prepare the ingredients

Once you have all that's necessary to prepare your recipe, place the ingredients directly inside the appliance or use a basket, a rack, or a pan to do so. To prevent sticking use parchment baking paper or simply spray the food with a little bit of oil. A word of caution is necessary here. Never over-stuff the chamber with too much food. It will not cook to an equal measure, and you may find yourself getting frustrated chewing under-cooked bits. If you're planning on cooking more, multiple rounds of air-frying may be necessary.

Set the temperature and time

Most of Air Fryers use pre-set modes depending on the type of recipe. You can adjust settings such as time and temperature manually to make the best use of your recipes.

Check food during cooking

Many recipes will require you to control from time to time the content of your fryer while cooking. This is to make sure everything gets cooked evenly. Normally all it takes is to shake or flip the food to distribute it. For some recipes, however, you'll need to turn the food around some time halfway through the cooking.

Cleaning time

Before you start cleaning, plug the air fryer off and let it cool down. Once it's ready, stick to instructions you got from the manufacturer and never scrub or use any other abrasive material on the inner surface of the chamber.

BREAKFAST RECIPES

1. Chicken Balls

Preparation time: 10 minutes

Cooking time: 8 minutes

Servings: 5

Ingredients:

- 8 oz. ground chicken

- 1 egg white

- 1 tablespoon dried parsley

- ½ teaspoon salt

- ½ teaspoon ground black pepper

- 2 tablespoons almond flour

- 1 tablespoon olive oil

- 1 teaspoon paprika

Directions:

1. Whisk the egg white and combine it with the ground chicken.

2. Sprinkle the chicken mixture with the dried parsley and salt.

3. Add ground black pepper and paprika.

4. Stir carefully using a spoon.

5. Using wet hands, make small balls from the ground chicken mixture.

6. Sprinkle each sausage ball with the almond flour.

7. Preheat the air fryer to 380 F.

8. Grease the air fryer basket tray with olive oil and place the sausage balls inside.

9. Cook for 8 minutes.

10. Turn halfway to crisp each side.

11. Serve hot.

Nutrition: calories 180 fat 11.8 fiber 1.5 carbs 2.9 protein 16.3

2. Tofu Egg Scramble

Preparation time: 15 minutes

Cooking time: 20 minutes

Servings: 5

Ingredients:

- 10 oz. tofu cheese

- 2 eggs

- 1 teaspoon chives

- 1 tablespoon apple cider vinegar

- ½ teaspoon salt

- 1 teaspoon ground white pepper

- ¼ teaspoon ground coriander

Directions:

1. Shred the tofu and sprinkle it with the apple cider vinegar, salt, ground white pepper, and ground coriander.

2. Mix and leave for 10 minutes to marinade.

3. Meanwhile, preheat the air fryer to 370 F.

4. Transfer the marinated tofu to the air fryer basket tray and cook for 13 minutes.

5. Meanwhile, crack the eggs in a bowl and whisk them.

6. When the tofu has cooked, pour the egg mixture in the shredded tofu cheese and stir with a spatula.

7. When the eggs start to firm place the air fryer basket tray in the air fryer and cook the dish for 7 minutes more.

8. Remove the cooked meal from the air fryer basket tray and serve.

Nutrition: calories 109 fat 6.7 fiber 1.4 carbs 2.9 protein 11.2

3. Flax & Hemp Porridge

Preparation time: 10 minutes

Cooking time: 15 minutes

Servings: 3

Ingredients:

- 2 tablespoon flax seeds
- 4 tablespoon hemp seeds
- 1 tablespoon butter
- ¼ teaspoon salt
- 1 teaspoon stevia
- 7 tablespoons almond milk
- ½ teaspoon ground ginger

Directions:

1. Place the flax seeds and hemp seeds in the air fryer basket.
2. Sprinkle the seeds with salt and ground ginger.
3. Combine the almond milk and stevia together. Stir the liquid and pour it into the seed mixture.
4. Add butter.
5. Preheat the air fryer to 370 F and cook the hemp seed porridge for 15 minutes.

6. Stir carefully after 10 minutes of cooking.

7. Remove the hem porridge from the air fryer basket tray and chill it for 3 minutes.

8. Transfer the porridge into serving bowls.

Nutrition: calories 196 fat 18.2 fiber 2.4 carbs 4.2 protein 5.1

4. Creamy Bacon Eggs

Preparation time: 10 minutes

Cooking time: 10 minutes

Servings: 4

Ingredients:

- 6 oz. bacon

- 4 eggs

- 5 tablespoons heavy cream

- 1 tablespoon butter

- 1 teaspoon paprika

- ½ teaspoon nutmeg

- 1 teaspoon salt

- 1 teaspoon ground black pepper

Directions:

1. Chop the bacon into small pieces and sprinkle it with salt.

2. Mix to combine and put in the air fryer basket.

3. Preheat the air fryer to 360 F and cook the bacon for 5 minutes.

4. Meanwhile, crack the eggs in a bowl and whisk them using a hand whisker.

5. Sprinkle the egg mixture with paprika, nutmeg, and ground black pepper.

6. Whisk egg mixture gently.

7. Toss the butter into the bacon and pour the egg mixture.

8. Add the heavy cream and cook for 2 minutes.

9. Stir the mixture with a spatula until you get scrambled eggs and cook for 3 minutes more.

10. Transfer onto serving plates.

Nutrition: calories 387 fat 32.1 fiber 0.4 carbs 2.3 protein 21.9

5. Cheddar Bacon Hash

Preparation time: 8 minutes

Cooking time: 8 minutes

Servings: 4

Ingredients:

- 1 zucchini

- 7 oz. bacon, cooked

- 4 oz. Cheddar cheese

- 2 tablespoon butter

- 1 teaspoon salt

- 1 teaspoon ground black pepper

- 1 teaspoon paprika

- 1 teaspoon cilantro

- 1 teaspoon ground thyme

Directions:

1. Chop the zucchini into the small cubes and sprinkle it with salt, ground black pepper, paprika, cilantro, and ground thyme.

2. Preheat the air fryer to 400 F and toss the butter into the air fryer basket tray.

3. Melt it and add the zucchini cubes.

4. Cook the zucchini for 5 minutes.

5. Meanwhile, shred Cheddar cheese.

6. Shake the zucchini cubes carefully and add the cooked bacon.

7. Sprinkle the zucchini mixture with the shredded cheese and cook it for 3 minutes more.

8. Transfer the breakfast hash in the serving bowls and stir.

Nutrition: calories 445 fat 36.1 fiber 1 carbs 3.5 protein 26.3

MAIN DISH

6. Sirloin with Garlic and Thyme

Preparation time: 5 minutes

Cooking time: 10 minutes

Servings: 4

Ingredients:

- 4 (5 oz. each) sirloin steak

- Steak Rub:

- 2 tablespoons. low-sodium steak sauce

- 2 tablespoons. olive oil

- 1 Tablespoon. freshly chopped thyme

- 1 teaspoon. minced garlic

- ½ teaspoon. ground coriander seeds

- ¼ teaspoon. kosher salt

- ¼ teaspoon. freshly ground black pepper

Directions:

1. Preheat Air Fryer to 360°F.

2. Mix together all steak rubs ingredients in a mixing bowl. Add the steak and rub with this mixture. Cover and let sit for 30 minutes inside the refrigerator.

3. Place steaks in the Air Fryer cooking basket. Cook for 8-10 minutes (medium rare) or 12-15 minutes (well-done).

4. Serve and enjoy!

Nutrition: Calories: 274 Fat: 12.2g Carbs: 0.7g Protein: 34.5 g

7. Yogurt Garlic Chicken

Preparation Time: 30 minutes

Cooking time: 60 minutes

Servings: 6

Ingredients:

- Pita bread rounds, halved (6 pieces)

- English cucumber, sliced thinly, w/ each slice halved (1 cup)

- Olive oil (3 tablespoons)

- Black pepper, freshly ground (1/2 teaspoon)

- Chicken thighs, skinless, boneless (20 ounces)

- Bell pepper, red, sliced into half-inch portions (1 piece)

- Garlic cloves, chopped finely (4 pieces)

- Cumin, ground (1/2 teaspoon)

- Red onion, medium, sliced into half-inch wedges (1 piece)

- Yogurt, plain, fat free (1/2 cup)

- Lemon juice (2 tablespoons)

- Salt (1 ½ teaspoons)

- Red pepper flakes, crushed (1/2 teaspoon)

- Allspice, ground (1/2 teaspoon)

- Bell pepper, yellow, sliced into half-inch portions (1 piece)

- Yogurt sauce

- Olive oil (2 tablespoons)

- Salt (1/4 teaspoon)

- Parsley, flat leaf, chopped finely (1 tablespoon)

- Yogurt, plain, fat free (1 cup)

- Lemon juice, fresh (1 tablespoon)

- Garlic clove, chopped finely (1 piece)

Directions:

1. Mix the yogurt (1/2 cup), garlic cloves (4 pieces), olive oil (1 tablespoon), salt (1 teaspoon), lemon juice (2 tablespoons), pepper (1/4 teaspoon), allspice, cumin, and pepper flakes. Stir in the chicken and coat well. Cover and marinate in the fridge for two hours.

2. Preheat the air fryer at 400 degrees Fahrenheit.

3. Grease a rimmed baking sheet (18x13-inch) with cooking spray.

4. Toss the bell peppers and onion with remaining olive oil (2 tablespoons), pepper (1/4 teaspoon), and salt (1/2 teaspoon).

5. Arrange veggies on the baking sheets left side and the marinated chicken thighs (drain first) on the right side. Cook in the air fryer for twenty-five to thirty minutes.

6. Mix the yogurt sauce ingredients.

7. Slice air-fried chicken into half-inch strips.

8. Top each pita round with chicken strips, roasted veggies, cucumbers, and yogurt sauce.

Nutrition: Calories 380 Fat 15.0 g Protein 26.0 g Carbohydrates 34.0 g

8. Lemony Parmesan Salmon

Preparation Time: 10 minutes

Cooking time: 25 minutes

Servings: 4

Ingredients:

- Butter, melted (2 tablespoons)

- Green onions, sliced thinly (2 tablespoons)

- Breadcrumbs, white, fresh (3/4 cup)

- Thyme leaves, dried (1/4 teaspoon)

- Salmon fillet, 1 ¼-pound (1 piece)

- Salt (1/4 teaspoon)

- Parmesan cheese, grated (1/4 cup)

- Lemon peel, grated (2 teaspoons)

Directions:

1. Preheat the air fryer at 350 degrees Fahrenheit.

2. Mist cooking spray onto a baking pan (shallow). Fill with pat-dried salmon. Brush salmon with butter (1 tablespoon) before sprinkling with salt.

3. Combine the breadcrumbs with onions, thyme, lemon peel, cheese, and remaining butter (1 tablespoon).

4. Cover salmon with the breadcrumb mixture. Air-fry for fifteen to twenty-five minutes.

Nutrition: Calories 290 Fat 16.0 g Protein 33.0 g Carbohydrates 4.0 g

9. Easiest Tuna Cobbler Ever

Preparation time: 15 minutes

Cooking time: 25 minutes

Servings: 4

Ingredients:

- Water, cold (1/3 cup)

- Tuna, canned, drained (10 ounces)

- Sweet pickle relish (2 tablespoons)

- Mixed vegetables, frozen (1 ½ cups)

- Soup, cream of chicken, condensed (10 ¾ ounces)

- Pimientos, sliced, drained (2 ounces)

- Lemon juice (1 teaspoon)

- Paprika

Directions:

1. Preheat the air fryer at 375 degrees Fahrenheit.

2. Mist cooking spray into a round casserole (1 ½ quarts).

3. Mix the frozen vegetables with milk, soup, lemon juice, relish, pimientos, and tuna in a saucepan. Cook for six to eight minutes over medium heat.

4. Fill the casserole with the tuna mixture.

5. Mix the biscuit mix with cold water to form a soft dough. Beat for half a minute before dropping by four spoonsful into the casserole.

6. Dust the dish with paprika before air-frying for twenty to twenty-five minute.

Nutrition: Calories 320 Fat 11.0 g Protein 28.0 g Carbohydrates 31.0 g

10.Deliciously Homemade Pork Buns

Preparation time: 20 minutes

Cooking time: 25 minutes

Servings: 8

Ingredients:

- Green onions, sliced thinly (3 pieces)

- Egg, beaten (1 piece)

- Pulled pork, diced, w/ barbecue sauce (1 cup)

- Buttermilk biscuits, refrigerated (16 1/3 ounces)

- Soy sauce (1 teaspoon)

Directions:

1. Preheat the air fryer at 325 degrees Fahrenheit.

2. Use parchment paper to line your baking sheet.

3. Combine pork with green onions.

4. Separate and press the dough to form 8 four-inch rounds.

5. Fill each biscuit round's center with two tablespoons of pork mixture. Cover with the dough edges and seal by pinching. Arrange the buns on the sheet and brush with a mixture of soy sauce and egg.

6. Cook in the air fryer for twenty to twenty-five minutes.

Nutrition: Calories 240 Fat 9.0 g Protein 8.0 g Carbohydrates 29.0 g

11. Mouthwatering Tuna Melts

Preparation time: 15 minutes

Cooking time: 20 minutes

Servings: 8

Ingredients:

- Salt (1/8 teaspoon)

- Onion, chopped (1/3 cup)

- Biscuits, refrigerated, flaky layers (16 1/3 ounces)

- Tuna, water packed, drained (10 ounces)

- Mayonnaise (1/3 cup)

- Pepper (1/8 teaspoon)

- Cheddar cheese, shredded (4 ounces)

- Tomato, chopped

- Sour cream

- Lettuce, shredded

Directions:

1. Preheat the air fryer at 325 degrees Fahrenheit.

2. Mist cooking spray onto a cookie sheet.

3. Mix tuna with mayonnaise, pepper, salt, and onion.

4. Separate dough so you have 8 biscuits; press each into 5-inch rounds.

5. Arrange 4 biscuit rounds on the sheet. Fill at the center with tuna mixture before topping with cheese. Cover with the remaining biscuit rounds and press to seal.

6. Air-fry for fifteen to twenty minutes. Slice each sandwich into halves. Serve each piece topped with lettuce, tomato, and sour cream.

Nutrition: Calories 320 Fat 18.0 g Protein 14.0 g Carbohydrates 27.0 g

SIDE DISHES

12. Onion Green Beans

Preparation time: 10 minutes

Cooking time: 12 minutes

Servings: 2

Ingredients:

- 11 oz. green beans
- 1 tablespoon onion powder
- 1 tablespoon olive oil
- ½ teaspoon salt
- ¼ teaspoon chili flakes

Directions:

1. Wash the green beans carefully and place them in the bowl.
2. Sprinkle the green beans with the onion powder, salt, chili flakes, and olive oil.
3. Shake the green beans carefully.
4. Preheat the air fryer to 400 F.

5. Put the green beans in the air fryer and cook for 8 minutes.

6. After this, shake the green beans and cook them for 4 minutes more at 400 F.

7. When the time is over – shake the green beans.

8. Serve the side dish and enjoy!

Nutrition: calories 1205, fat 7.2, fiber 5.5, carbs 13.9, protein 3.2

13.Mozzarella Radish Salad

Preparation time: 10 minutes

Cooking time: 20 minutes

Servings: 2

Ingredients:

- 8 oz. radish

- 4 oz. Mozzarella

- 1 teaspoon balsamic vinegar

- ½ teaspoon salt

- 1 tablespoon olive oil

- 1 teaspoon dried oregano

Directions:

1. Wash the radish carefully and cut it into the halves.

2. Preheat the air fryer to 360 F.

3. Put the radish halves in the air fryer basket.

4. Sprinkle the radish with the salt and olive oil.

5. Cook the radish for 20 minutes.

6. Shake the radish after 10 minutes of cooking.

7. When the time is over – transfer the radish to the serving plate.

8. Chop Mozzarella roughly.

9. Sprinkle the radish with Mozzarella, balsamic vinegar, and dried oregano.

10. Stir it gently with the help of 2 forks.

11. Serve it immediately.

Nutrition: calories 241, fat 17.2, fiber 2.1, carbs 6.4, protein 16.9

14. Cremini Mushroom Satay

Preparation time: 10 minutes

Cooking time: 6 minutes

Servings: 2

Ingredients:

- 7 oz. cremini mushrooms
- 2 tablespoon coconut milk
- 1 tablespoon butter
- 1 teaspoon chili flakes
- ½ teaspoon balsamic vinegar
- ½ teaspoon curry powder
- ½ teaspoon white pepper

Directions:

1. Wash the mushrooms carefully.
2. Then sprinkle the mushrooms with the chili flakes, curry powder, and white pepper.
3. Preheat the air fryer to 400 F.
4. Toss the butter in the air fryer basket and melt it.
5. Put the mushrooms in the air fryer and cook for 2 minutes.

6. Shake the mushrooms well and sprinkle with the coconut milk and balsamic vinegar.

7. Cook the mushrooms for 4 minutes more at 400 F.

8. Then skewer the mushrooms on the wooden sticks and serve.

9. Enjoy!

Nutrition: calories 116, fat 9.5, fiber 1.3, carbs 5.6, protein 3

15.Eggplant Ratatouille

Preparation time: 15 minutes

Cooking time: 15 minutes

Servings: 2

Ingredients:

- 1 eggplant
- 1 sweet yellow pepper
- 3 cherry tomatoes
- 1/3 white onion, chopped
- ½ teaspoon garlic clove, sliced
- 1 teaspoon olive oil
- ½ teaspoon ground black pepper
- ½ teaspoon Italian seasoning

Directions:

1. Preheat the air fryer to 360 F.
2. Peel the eggplants and chop them.
3. Put the chopped eggplants in the air fryer basket.
4. Chop the cherry tomatoes and add them to the air fryer basket.
5. Then add chopped onion, sliced garlic clove, olive oil, ground black pepper, and Italian seasoning.

6. Chop the sweet yellow pepper roughly and add it to the air fryer basket.

7. Shake the vegetables gently and cook for 15 minutes.

8. Stir the meal after 8 minutes of cooking.

9. Transfer the cooked ratatouille in the serving plates.

10. Enjoy!

Nutrition: calories 149, fat 3.7, fiber 11.7, carbs 28.9, protein 5.1

SEAFOOD RECIPES

16.Perfect Salmon Fillets

Preparation Time: 10 minutes

Cooking Time: 15 minutes

Servings: 2

Ingredients:

- 2 salmon fillets
- 1/2 teaspoon garlic powder
- 1/4 cup plain yogurt
- 1 teaspoon fresh lemon juice
- 1 tablespoon. fresh dill, chopped
- 1 lemon, sliced
- Pepper
- Salt

Directions:

1. Place lemon slices into the air fryer basket.

45

2. Season salmon with pepper and salt and place on top of lemon slices into the air fryer basket.

3. Cook salmon at 330 F for 15 minutes.

4. Meanwhile, in a bowl, mix together yogurt, garlic powder, lemon juice, dill, pepper, and salt.

5. Place salmon on serving plate and top with yogurt mixture.

6. Serve and enjoy.

Nutrition: Calories 195 Fat 7 g Carbohydrates 6 g Sugar 2 g Protein 24 g Cholesterol 65 mg

17.Nutritious Salmon

Preparation Time: 10 minutes

Cooking Time: 10 minutes

Servings: 2

Ingredients:

- 2 salmon fillets

- 1 tablespoon. olive oil

- 1/4 teaspoon ground cardamom

- 1/2 teaspoon paprika

- Salt

Directions:

1. Preheat the air fryer to 350 F.

2. Coat salmon fillets with olive oil and season with paprika, cardamom, and salt and place into the air fryer basket.

3. Cook salmon for 10-12 minutes. Turn halfway through.

Nutrition: Calories 160 Fat 1 g Carbohydrates 1 g Sugar 0.5 g Protein 22 g Cholesterol 60 mg

18.Shrimp Scampi

Preparation Time: 10 minutes

Cooking Time: 10 minutes

Servings: 4

Ingredients:

- 1 lb. shrimp, peeled and deveined

- 10 garlic cloves, peeled

- 2 tablespoon. olive oil

- 1 fresh lemon, cut into wedges

- 1/4 cup parmesan cheese, grated

- 2 tablespoon. butter, melted

Directions:

1. Preheat the air fryer to 370 F.

2. Mix together shrimp, lemon wedges, olive oil, and garlic cloves in a bowl.

3. Pour shrimp mixture into the air fryer pan and place into the air fryer and cook for 10 minutes.

4. Drizzle with melted butter and sprinkle with parmesan cheese.

5. Serve and enjoy.

Nutrition: Calories 295 Fat 17 g Carbohydrates 4 g Sugar 0.1 g Protein 29 g Cholesterol 260 mg

19.Lemon Chili Salmon

Preparation Time: 10 minutes

Cooking Time: 17 minutes

Servings: 4

Ingredients:

- 2 lbs. salmon fillet, skinless and boneless
- 2 lemon juice
- 1 orange juice
- 1 tablespoon. olive oil
- 1 bunch fresh dill
- 1 chili, sliced
- Pepper
- Salt

Directions:

1. Preheat the air fryer to 325 F.
2. Place salmon fillets in air fryer baking pan and drizzle with olive oil, lemon juice, and orange juice.
3. Sprinkle chili slices over salmon and season with pepper and salt.
4. Place pan in the air fryer and cook for 15-17 minutes.
5. Garnish with dill and serve.

Nutrition: Calories 339 Fat 17.5 g Carbohydrates 2 g Sugar 2 g Protein

44 g Cholesterol 100 mg

POULTRY RECIPES

20. Rosemary Turkey Breast with Maple Mustard Glaze

Preparation time: 20 minutes

Cooking time: 30 minutes

Servings: 7

Ingredients:

- 1 tablespoon. vegan butter

- 1 tablespoon. stone-ground brown mustard

- ¼ C. pure maple syrup

- 1 teaspoon. crushed pepper

- 2 teaspoon. salt

- ½ teaspoon. dried rosemary

- 2 minced garlic cloves

- ¼ C. olive oil

- 2.5 pounds' turkey breast loin

Directions:

1. Mix pepper, salt, rosemary, garlic, and olive oil together. Spread herb mixture over turkey breast. Cover and chill 2 hours or overnight to marinade.

2. Make sure to remove from fridge about half an hour before cooking.

3. Ensure your air fryer is greased well and preheated to 400 degrees. Place loin into the fryer and cook 20 minutes.

4. Open fryer and spoon on butter mixture over turkey. Cook another 10 minutes.

5. Remove turkey from the fryer and let rest 5-10 minutes before attempting to slice.

6. Slice against the grain and enjoy!

Nutrition: Calories: 278 Fat: 15g Protein: 29g Sugar: 7g

21.Mexican Chicken Burgers

Preparation time: 5 minutes

Cooking time: 20 minutes

Servings: 8

Ingredients:

- 1 jalapeno pepper

- 1 teaspoon. cayenne pepper

- 1 tablespoon. mustard powder

- 1 tablespoon. oregano

- 1 tablespoon. thyme

- 3 tablespoon. smoked paprika

- 1 beaten egg

- 1 small head of cauliflower

- 4 chicken breasts

Directions:

1. Ensure your air fryer is preheated to 350 degrees.

2. Add seasonings to a blender. Slice cauliflower into florets and add to blender.

3. Pulse till mixture resembles that of breadcrumbs.

4. Take out ¾ of cauliflower mixture and add to a bowl. Set to the side. In another bowl, beat your egg and set to the side.

5. Remove skin and bones from chicken breasts and add to blender with remaining cauliflower mixture. Season with pepper and salt.

6. Take out mixture and form into burger shapes. Roll each patty in cauliflower crumbs, then the egg, and back into crumbs again.

7. Place coated patties into the air fryer, cooking 20 minutes.

8. Flip over at 10-minute mark. They are done when crispy!

Nutrition: Calories: 234 Fat: 18g Protein: 24g Sugar: 1g

MEAT RECIPES

22. Mediterranean-Style Beef Steak and Zucchini

Preparation time: 8 minutes

Cooking time: 12 minutes

Servings: 4

Ingredients:

- 1 ½ pounds beef steak

- 1-pound zucchini

- 1 teaspoon dried rosemary

- 1 teaspoon dried basil

- 1 teaspoon dried oregano

- 2 tablespoons extra-virgin olive oil

- 2 tablespoons fresh chives, chopped

Directions:

1. Start by preheating your Air Fryer to 400 degrees F.

2. Toss the steak and zucchini with the spices and olive oil. Transfer to the cooking basket and cook for 6 minutes.

3. Now, shale the basket and cook another 6 minutes. Serve immediately garnished with fresh chives. Enjoy!

Nutrition: 396 Calories; 20.4g Fat; 3.5g Carbs; 47.8g Protein; 0.1g Sugars

23. New York Strip with Mustard Butter

Preparation time: 6 minutes

Cooking time: 14 minutes

Servings: 4

Ingredients:

- 1 tablespoon peanut oil

- 2 pounds New York Strip

- 1 teaspoon cayenne pepper

- Sea salt and freshly cracked black pepper, to taste

- 1/2 stick butter, softened

- 1 teaspoon whole-grain mustard

- 1/2 teaspoon honey

Directions:

1. Rub the peanut oil all over the steak; season with cayenne pepper, salt, and black pepper.

2. Cook in the preheated Air Fryer at 400 degrees F for 7 minutes; turn over and cook an additional 7 minutes.

3. Meanwhile, prepare the mustard butter by whisking the butter, whole-grain mustard, and honey.

4. Serve the roasted New York Strip dolloped with the mustard butter.

   Bon appétit!

Nutrition: 459 Calories; 27.4g Fat; 2.5g Carbs; 48.3g Protein; 1.4g

Sugars

24. Scotch Fillet with Sweet 'n' Sticky Sauce

Preparation time: 10 minutes

Cooking time: 30 minutes

Servings: 4

Ingredients:

- 2 pounds' scotch fillet, sliced into strips

- 4 tablespoons tortilla chips, crushed

- 2 green onions, chopped

Sauce:

- 1 tablespoon butter

- 2 garlic cloves, minced

- 1/2 teaspoon dried rosemary

- 1/2 teaspoon dried dill

- 1/2 cup beef broth

- 1 tablespoons fish sauce

- 2 tablespoons honey

Directions:

1. Start by preheating your Air Fryer to 390 degrees F.

2. Coat the beef strips with the crushed tortilla chips on all sides. Spritz with cooking spray on all sides and transfer them to the cooking basket.

3. Cook for 30 minutes, shaking the basket every 10 minutes.

4. Meanwhile, heat the sauce ingredient in a saucepan over medium-high heat. Bring to a boil and reduce the heat; cook until the sauce has thickened slightly.

5. Add the steak to the sauce; let it sit approximately 8 minutes. Serve over the hot egg noodles if desired.

Nutrition: 556 Calories; 17.9g Fat; 25.8g Carbs; 60g Protein; 10.4g Sugars

25. Roasted Ribeye with Garlic Mayo

Preparation time: 5 minutes

Cooking time: 15 minutes

Servings: 3

Ingredients:

- 1 ½ pounds ribeye, bone-in

- 1 tablespoon butter, room temperature

- Salt, to taste

- 1/2 teaspoon crushed black pepper

- 1/2 teaspoon dried dill

- 1/2 teaspoon cayenne pepper

- 1/2 teaspoon garlic powder

- 1/2 teaspoon onion powder

- 1 teaspoon ground coriander

- 3 tablespoons mayonnaise

- 1 teaspoon garlic, minced

Directions:

1. Start by preheating your Air Fryer to 400 degrees F.

2. Pat dry the ribeye and rub it with softened butter on all sides. Sprinkle with seasonings and transfer to the cooking basket.

---

3. Cook in the preheated Air Fryer for 15 minutes, flipping them halfway through the cooking time.

4. In the meantime, simply mix the mayonnaise with garlic and place in the refrigerator until ready to serve. Bon appétit!

Nutrition: 437 Calories; 24.8g Fat; 1.8g Carbs; 51g Protein; 0.1g Sugars

26.   Crustless Beef and Cheese Tart

Preparation time: 6 minutes

Cooking time: 19 minutes

Servings: 4

Ingredients:

- 1 tablespoon canola oil

- 1 onion, finely chopped

- 2 fresh garlic cloves, minced

- 1/2-pound ground chuck

- 1/2-pound Chorizo sausage, crumbled

- 1 cup pasta sauce

- Sea salt, to taste

- 1/4 teaspoon ground black pepper

- 1/2 teaspoon red pepper flakes, crushed

- 1 cup cream cheese, room temperature

- 1/2 cup Swiss cheese, shredded

- 1 egg

- 1/2 cup crackers, crushed

Directions:

1. Start by preheating your Air Fryer to 370 degrees F.

2. Grease a baking pan with canola oil.

3. Add the onion, garlic, ground chuck, sausage, pasta sauce, salt, black pepper, and red pepper. Cook for 9 minutes.

4. In the meantime, combine cheese with egg. Place the cheese-egg mixture over the beef mixture.

5. Sprinkle with crushed crackers and cook for 10 minutes. Serve warm and enjoy!

Nutrition: 572 Calories; 44.6g Fat; 16.2g Carbs; 28.1g Protein; 8.9g Sugars

27. Pork Wonton Wonderful

Preparation Time: 10 Minutes

Cooking Time: 25 Minutes

Servings: 3

Ingredients:

- 8 wanton wrappers (Leasa brand works great, though any will do)

- ounces of raw minced pork

- 1 medium-sized green apple

- 1 cup of water, for wetting the wanton wrappers

- 1 tablespoon of vegetable oil

- ½ tablespoon of oyster sauce

- 1 tablespoon of soy sauce

- Large pinch of ground white pepper

Directions:

1. Cover the basket of the Smart Air Fryer Oven with a lining of tin foil, leaving the edges uncovered to allow air to circulate through the basket. Preheat the air fryer to 350 degrees.

2. In a small mixing bowl, combine the oyster sauce, soy sauce, and white pepper, then add in the minced pork and stir thoroughly.

3. Cover and set in the fridge to marinate for at least 15 minutes. Core the apple, and slice into small cubes – smaller than bite-sized chunks.

4. Add the apples to the marinating meat mixture, and combine thoroughly. Spread the wonton wrappers, and fill each with a large spoonful of the filling.

5. Wrap the wontons into triangles, so that the wrappers fully cover the filling, and seal with a drop of the water.

6. Coat each filled and wrapped wonton thoroughly with the vegetable oil, to help ensure a nice crispy fry. Place the wontons on the foil-lined air-fryer basket.

7. Set the Smart Air Fryer Oven timer to 25 minutes. Halfway through cooking time, shake the handle of the air fryer basket vigorously to jostle the wontons and ensure even frying.

8. After 25 minutes, when the Smart Air Fryer Oven shuts off, the wontons will be crispy golden-brown on the outside and juicy and delicious on the inside.

9. Serve directly from the air fryer basket and enjoy while hot.

Nutrition: Calories: 242; Fat: 12g; Protein:28g; Sugar:4g

28.   Cilantro-Mint Pork BBQ Thai Style

Preparation Time: 5 Minutes

Cooking Time: 15 Minutes **Servings:** 3

Ingredients:

- 1 minced hot Chile

- 1 minced shallot

- 1-pound ground pork

- 2 tablespoons fish sauce

- 2 tablespoons lime juice

- 3 tablespoons basil

- tablespoons chopped mint

- tablespoons cilantro

Directions:

1. In a shallow dish, mix well all Ingredients with hands. Form into 1-inch ovals. Thread ovals in skewers. Place on skewer rack in air fryer. For 15 minutes, cook on 360°F. Halfway through cooking time, turnover skewers. If needed, cook in batches. Serve and enjoy.

Nutrition: Calories: 455; Fat: 31.5g; Protein:40.4g

VEGETABLE RECIPES

29. Fried Zucchini

Preparation time: 10 minutes

Cooking time: 8 minutes

Servings: 4

Ingredients:

- 2 medium zucchinis, cut into strips 19 mm thick

- 60g all-purpose flour

- 12g of salt

- 2g black pepper

- 2 beaten eggs

- 15 ml of milk

- 84g Italian seasoned breadcrumbs

- 25g grated Parmesan cheese

- Nonstick Spray Oil

- Ranch sauce, to serve

Directions:

1. Cut the zucchini into strips 19 mm thick.

2. Mix with the flour, salt, and pepper on a plate. Mix the eggs and milk in a separate dish. Put breadcrumbs and Parmesan cheese in another dish.

3. Cover each piece of zucchini with flour, then dip them in egg and pass them through the crumbs. Leave aside.

4. Preheat the air fryer, set it to 175°C.

5. Place the covered zucchini in the preheated air fryer and spray with oil spray. Set the timer to 8 minutes and press Start / Pause.

6. Be sure to shake the baskets in the middle of cooking.

7. Serve with tomato sauce or ranch sauce.

Nutrition: Calories: 68 Carbs: 2 g Fat: 11 g Protein: 4 g Fiber: 143g

30.   Fried Avocado

Preparation time: 15 minutes

Cooking time: 10 minutes

Servings: 2

Ingredients:

- 2 avocados cut into wedges 25 mm thick

- 50g Pan crumbs bread

- 2g garlic powder

- 2g onion powder

- 1g smoked paprika

- 1g cayenne pepper

- Salt and pepper to taste

- 60g all-purpose flour

- 2 eggs, beaten

- Nonstick Spray Oil

- Tomato sauce or ranch sauce, to serve

Directions:

1. Cut the avocados into 25 mm thick pieces.

2. Combine the crumbs, garlic powder, onion powder, smoked paprika, cayenne pepper and salt in a bowl.

3. Separate each wedge of avocado in the flour, then dip the beaten eggs and stir in the breadcrumb mixture.

4. Preheat the air fryer.

5. Place the avocados in the preheated air fryer baskets, spray with oil spray and cook at 205°C for 10 minutes. Turn the fried avocado halfway through cooking and sprinkle with cooking oil.

6. Serve with tomato sauce or ranch sauce.

Nutrition: Calories: 123 Carbs: 2 g Fat: 11 g Protein: 4 g Fiber: 0 g

31.Vegetables in air Fryer

Preparation time: 20 minutes

Cooking time: 30 minutes

Servings: 2

Ingredients:

- 2 potatoes
- 1 zucchini
- 1 onion
- 1 red pepper
- 1 green pepper

Directions:

- Cut the potatoes into slices.
- Cut the onion into rings.
- Cut the zucchini slices
- Cut the peppers into strips.
- Put all the ingredients in the bowl and add a little salt, ground pepper and some extra virgin olive oil.
- Mix well.
- Pass to the basket of the air fryer.
- Select 1600C, 30 minutes.

- Check that the vegetables are to your liking.

Nutrition: Calories: 135 Carbs: 2 g Fat: 11 g Protein: 4 g Fiber: 05g

32. Crispy Rye Bread Snacks with Guacamole and Anchovies

Preparation time: 10 minutes

Cooking time: 10 minutes

Servings: 4

Ingredients:

- 4 slices of rye bread

- Guacamole

- Anchovies in oil

Directions:

1. Cut each slice of bread into 3 strips of bread.

2. Place in the basket of the air fryer, without piling up, and we go in batches giving it the touch you want to give it. You can select 1800C, 10 minutes.

3. When you have all the crusty rye bread strips, put a layer of guacamole on top, whether homemade or commercial.

4. In each bread, place 2 anchovies on the guacamole.

Nutrition: Calories: 180 Carbs: 4 g Fat: 11 g Protein: 4 g Fiber: 09 g

33. Mushrooms Stuffed with Tomato

Preparation time: 5 minutes

Cooking time: 50 minutes

Servings: 4

Ingredients:

- 8 large mushrooms

- 250g of minced meat

- 4 cloves of garlic

- Extra virgin olive oil

- Salt

- Ground pepper

- Flour, beaten egg and breadcrumbs

- Frying oil

- Fried Tomato Sauce

Directions:

1. Remove the stem from the mushrooms and chop it. Peel the garlic and chop. Put some extra virgin olive oil in a pan and add the garlic and mushroom stems.

2. Sauté and add the minced meat. Sauté well until the meat is well cooked and season.

3. Fill the mushrooms with the minced meat.

4. Press well and take the freezer for 30 minutes.

5. Pass the mushrooms with flour, beaten egg and breadcrumbs. Beaten egg and breadcrumbs.

6. Place the mushrooms in the basket of the air fryer.

7. Select 20 minutes, 1800C.

8. Distribute the mushrooms once cooked in the dishes.

9. Heat the tomato sauce and cover the stuffed mushrooms.

Nutrition: Calories: 160 Carbs: 2 g Fat: 11 g Protein: 4 g Fiber: 0 g

34. Air Fryer Oreo Cookies

Preparation Time: 5 Minutes

Cooking Time: 5 Minutes

servings: 9

Ingredients:

- Pancake Mix: ½ cup

- Water: ½ cup

- Cooking spray

- Chocolate sandwich cookies: 9 (e.g. Oreo)

- Confectioners' sugar: 1 tablespoon, or to taste

Directions:

1. Blend the pancake mixture with the water until well mixed.

2. Line the parchment paper on the basket of an air fryer. Spray nonstick cooking spray on parchment paper.

3. Dip each cookie into the mixture of the pancake and place it in the basket. Make sure they do not touch; if possible, cook in batches.

4. The air fryer is preheated to 400 degrees F (200 degrees C). Add basket and cook for 4 to 5 minutes; flip until golden brown, 2 to 3 more minutes. Sprinkle the sugar over the cookies and serve.

Nutrition: Calories 77 Fat 2.1 g Sodium 156 mg Carbohydrates 13.7 g

Protein 1.2 g

35. Air Fried Butter Cake

Preparation Time: 10 Minutes

Cooking: 15 Minutes

Servings: 4

Ingredients:

- Cooking spray

- 7 Tablespoons of butter, at ambient temperature

- White sugar: ¼ cup plus 2 tablespoons

- 1 Ok.

- All-purpose flour: 1 2/3 cups

- Salt: 1 pinch or to taste

- Milk: 6 tablespoons

Directions:

1. Preheat an air fryer to 350 F (180 C). Spray the cooking spray on a tiny fluted tube pan.

2. Take a large bowl and add ¼ cup butter and 2 tablespoons of sugar in it.

3. Take an electric mixer to beat the sugar and butter until smooth and fluffy. Stir in salt and flour. Stir in the milk and thoroughly combine

batter. Move batter to the prepared saucepan; use a spoon back to level the surface.

4. Place the pan inside the basket of the air fryer. Set the timer within 15 minutes. Bake the batter until a toothpick comes out clean when inserted into the cake.

5. Turn the cake out of the saucepan and allow it to cool for about five minutes.

Nutrition: Calories 470 Fat 22.4 g Cholesterol 102 mg Sodium 210 mg Carbohydrates 59.7 g Protein 7.9 g

36.   Chocolate chip cookies

Preparation Time: 15 minutes

Cooking Time: 5 minutes

Servings: 18

Ingredients:

- Unsalted butter: 2 sticks (1 cup)

- Dark brown sugar: ¾ cup

- ¾ tablespoon of dark brown sugar

- Vanilla extract: 2 tablespoon

- 2 Big Eggs

- Kosher salt: 1 teaspoon

- Baking soda: 1 teaspoon

- All-purpose flour: 2 1/3 cups

- 2 Cups of chocolate chips

- Chopped walnuts: 3/4 cups

- Cooking spray

- Flaky sea salt, for garnish (optional)

Directions:

1. Take a large bowl and add unsalted butter in it. Beat the butter with an electric hand mixer. Add 3/4 cup of granulated sugar with 3/4 cup of dark brown sugar and beat at normal speed for 2 to 3 minutes.

2. Add 1 spoonful of vanilla extract, 2 large eggs and 1 tablespoon of kosher salt, and beat until mixed. Add in increments 1 tablespoon baking soda and 2 1/3 cups of all-purpose flour, stirring until it is just mixed.

3. Add 2 cups of chocolate chip chunks and 3/4 cup of chopped walnuts and stir until well combined with a rubber spatula.

4. Preheat the air Fryer to bake at 350°F and set aside for 5 minutes. Line the air fryer racks with parchment paper, making sure to leave space for air to circulate on all sides.

5. Drop the dough's 2-tablespoon scoops onto the racks, spacing them 1 "apart. Gently flatten each scoop to form a cookie.

6. If you like, sprinkle with flaky sea salt. Bake for about 5 minutes, until golden brown. Remove the air fryer's racks and set it to cool for 3 to 5 minutes. Repeat with leftover dough. Serve warm.

Nutrition: Calories: 330 Fat: 17.5 g Saturated: 8.5 g Carbs: 42.9 g Fiber: 1.9 g Sugars: 28.0 g Protein: 4.0 g Sodium: 172.1 mg

37. Air Fryer S'mores

Preparation Time: 5 Minutes

Cooking time: 1 minutes

Servings: 4

Ingredients:

- Four graham crackers (each half split to make 2 squares, for a total of 8 squares)

- 8 Squares of Hershey's chocolate bar, broken into squares

- 4 Marshmallows

Directions:

1. Take deliberate steps. Air-fryers use hot air for cooking food. Marshmallows are light and fluffy, and this should keep the marshmallows from flying around the basket if you follow these steps.

2. Put 4 squares of graham crackers on a basket of the air fryer.

3. Place 2 squares of chocolate bars on each cracker.

4. Place back the basket in the air fryer and fry on air at 390 °F for 1 minute. It is barely long enough for the chocolate to melt. Remove basket from air fryer.

5. Top with a marshmallow over each cracker. Throw the marshmallow down a little bit into the melted chocolate. This will help to make the marshmallow stay over the chocolate.

6. Put back the basket in the air fryer and fry at 390 °F for 2 minutes. (The marshmallows should be puffed up and browned at the tops.)

7. Using tongs to carefully remove each cracker from the basket of the air fryer and place it on a platter. Top each marshmallow with another square of graham crackers.

8. Enjoy it right away!

Nutrition: Calories: 330 Fat: 17.5 g Saturated: 8.5 g Carbs: 42.9 g Fiber: 1.9 g Sugars: 28.0 g Protein: 4.0 g Sodium: 172.1 mg

38. Double-glazed Cinnamon Biscuit Bites

Preparation Time: 25 Minutes

Cooking time: 12 minutes

Servings 8

Ingredients:

- All-purpose flour: 2/3 cup (approx. 2 7/8 oz.)

- 1/4 teaspoon cinnamon

- 2 tablespoons of granulated sugar

- 1 teaspoon baking powder

- 1/4 teaspoon kosher salt

- Whole-wheat flour: 2/3 cup (approx. 2 2/3 oz.)

- 4 tablespoons of cold salted butter, cut into small pieces

- Whole milk: 1/3 cup

- Cooking spray

- Powdered sugar: 2 cups (approx. 8 oz.)

- Water: 3 tablespoons

Directions:

1. Take a medium-sized bowl, whisk the flours together, granulated sugar, baking powder, cinnamon, and salt.

2. Add butter; use 2 knives or a pastry cutter to cut into mixture until butter is well mixed with flour and mixture resembles coarse cornmeal. Add milk, then stir until dough forms a ball. Place the dough on a floured surface and knead for about 30 seconds until it is smooth, forming a cohesive disk. Cut the dough into 16 pieces equal to each other. Wrap each piece gently into a smooth ball. Coat air fryer basket with spray to cook well. Place 8 balls in a basket, leave room between each; spray the donut balls with the spray for cooking. Cook for 10 to 12 minutes, at 350 ° F until browned and puffed. Remove the donut balls gently from the basket, and place over foil on a wire rack. Keep it cool for 5 minutes. Repeat the same process with remaining donut balls. Whisk the caster sugar and water together until smooth in a medium cup. Spoon half of the glaze gently over donut sticks. Let cool for 5 minutes; glaze again, allowing excess to drip away.

Nutrition: Calories 325 Fat 7 g Sat fat 4 g Unsaturated fat 3 g Protein 8 g Carbohydrate 60 g Fiber 5 g Added Sugars 18 g Calcium 17 g Sodium 67 mg Calcium 10

FAST FOOD

39. Pizza Dogs

Preparation time: 10 minutes

Cooking time: 17 minutes

Servings: 2

Ingredients:

- 2 hot dogs

- 4 slices pepperoni, halved

- ½ cup pizza sauce

- 2 hot dog buns

- ¼ cup shredded mozzarella cheese

- 2 teaspoon sliced olives

Directions:

1. Ensure that your air fryer is preheated to 390 F.

2. Cut four slits into each hot dog, and place them into the basket of the air fryer.

3. Allow cooking for 3 minutes before withdrawing onto a cutting board using tongs.

4. Put a pepperoni half in each of the slits in the hot dogs. Divide the pizza sauce between the buns, and fill with the olives, hot dogs, and mozzarella cheese.

5. Place the hot dogs in the basket of the air fryer and allow to cook, again.

6. Remove when the cheese is melted, and the buns appear crisp - this takes about 2 minutes.

Nutrition: calories 156, fat 2, fiber 19, carbs 14, protein 28

SALAD RECIPES

40.   Potato Salad

Preparation time: 10 minutes

Cooking Time: 40 minutes

Servings: 6

Ingredients:

- 4 Russet potatoes

- 1 tablespoon olive oil

- Salt, as required

- 3 hard-boiled eggs, peeled and chopped

- 1 cup celery, chopped

- ½ cup red onion, chopped

- 1 tablespoon prepared mustard

- ¼ teaspoon celery salt

- ¼ teaspoon garlic salt

- ¼ cup mayonnaise

Directions:

1. Set the temperature of air fryer to 390 degrees F. Grease an air fryer basket.

2. With a fork, prick the potatoes.

3. Drizzle with oil and rub with the salt.

4. Arrange potatoes into the prepared air fryer basket.

5. Air fry for about 35-40 minutes.

6. Remove from air fryer and transfer the potatoes into a bowl.

7. Set aside to cool.

8. After cooling, chop the potatoes.

9. In a serving bowl, add the potatoes and remaining ingredients and gently, mix them well.

10. Refrigerate to chill before serving.

11. Serve.

Nutrition: Calories: 196 Carbohydrate: 26.5g Protein: 5.6g Fat: 8.1g Sugar: 3.1g Sodium: 18`0mg

SNACK & APPETIZERS

RECIPES

41.Rosemary Carrot Fries

Preparation time: 10 minutes.

Cooking Time: 12 minutes.

Servings: 2

Ingredients:

- 1 large carrot, peeled and cut into sticks

- 1 tablespoon fresh rosemary, chopped finely

- 1 tablespoon olive oil

- ¼ teaspoon cayenne pepper

- Salt and ground black pepper, as required

Directions:

1. In a bowl, add all the carrot fries **Ingredients:** and mix well. Transfer the carrots to the Air fryer basket inside the Instant Pot. Put on the Instant Air Fryer lid and cook on Air Fry mode for 12 minutes at 390 degrees F. Once done, remove the lid and serve warm.

Nutrition: calories: 149 Protein: 5g Carbs: 12.8g Fat: 11.9g

42. Butternut Squash Fries

Preparation time: 10 minutes.

Cooking Time: 30 minutes.

Servings: 2

Ingredients:

- 14 oz. butternut squash, peeled, and cut into strips

- 2 teaspoons olive oil

- ½ teaspoon ground cinnamon

- ½ teaspoon red chili powder

- ¼ teaspoon garlic salt

- Salt and black pepper, as needed

Directions:

1. In a bowl, add all the fries **Ingredients:** and toss to coat well. Transfer the squash fries to the Air Fryer basket inside the Instant Pot.

2. Put on the Instant Air Fryer lid and cook on Air Fry mode for 30 minutes at 400 degrees F. Once done, remove the lid and serve warm.

Nutrition: calories: 113 Protein: 2g Carbs: 13g Fat: 4g

43.   Breaded Pickle Fries

Preparation time: 10 minutes.

Cooking Time: 15 minutes.

Servings: 4

Ingredients:

- 1 (16oz.) jar spicy dill pickle spears, drained and pat dried

- 3/4 cup all-purpose flour

- ½ teaspoon paprika

- 1 egg, beaten

- ¼ cup milk

- 1 cup panko breadcrumbs

- Nonstick cooking spray

Directions:

1. In a medium-sized dish, mix together the flour, and paprika. In a second dish, place the milk and egg and mix well. In a third dish, put the breadcrumbs.

2. Coat the pickle spears with flour mixture, then dip into the egg mixture, and finally, coat evenly with the breadcrumbs.

3. Now, spray the pickle spears evenly with cooking spray. And place them Air fryer basket inside the Instant pot.

4. Put on the Instant Air Fryer lid and cook on Air Fry mode for 15 minutes at 400 degrees F. Once done, remove the lid and serve warm.

Nutrition: calories: 179 Protein: 10.2g Carbs: 13.7g Fat: 29.7g

44.   Buttered Corn Cob

Preparation time: 10 minutes.

Cooking Time: 20 minutes.

Servings: 2

Ingredients:

- 2 corn on the cob

- Salt and black pepper, as needed

- 2 tablespoons butter, softened and divided

Directions:

1. Sprinkle the cobs evenly with salt and black pepper. Then, rub with 1 tablespoon of butter.

2. With 1 piece of foil, wrap each cob. Place the Corn Cob in the Air fryer basket inside the Instant Pot.

3. Put on the Instant Air Fryer lid and cook on Air Fry mode for 20 minutes at 320 degrees F. Once done, remove the lid and serve warm.

Nutrition: calories: 168 protein: 7.2g Carbs: 72.8g Fat: 1.2g

45. Polenta Bars

Preparation time: 10 minutes.

Cooking Time: 6 minutes.

Servings: 4

Ingredients:

- 1 tablespoon oil
- 2½ cups cooked polenta
- Salt, to taste
- ¼ cup Parmesan cheese

Directions:

1. Place the polenta in a lightly greased baking pan. With a plastic wrap, cover, and refrigerate for about 1 hour or until set. Remove from the refrigerator and cut into serving-sized slices. Sprinkle with salt. Place the Polenta bars in the Air Fryer basket inside the Instant Pot.

2. Put on the Instant Air Fryer lid and cook on Air Fry mode for 6 minutes at 350 degrees F. Once done, remove the lid and garnish with cheese. Serve warm.

Nutrition: calories: 101 Protein: 8.8g Carbs: 25g Fat: 2.2g

46.   Eggplant Crisps

Preparation time: 10 minutes.

Cooking Time: 8 minutes.

Servings: 4

Ingredients:

- 1 medium eggplant, peeled and cut into ½inch round slices

- Salt, as required

- ½ cup all-purpose flour

- 2 eggs, beaten

- 1 cup Italian style breadcrumbs

- ¼ cup olive oil

Directions:

1. In a colander, add the eggplant slices and sprinkle with salt. Set aside for about 45 minutes.

2. With paper towels, pat dry the eggplant slices. In a shallow dish, place the flour. Crack the eggs in a second dish and beat well.

3. In a third dish, mix together the oil, and breadcrumbs. Coat each eggplant slice with flour, then dip into beaten eggs, and finally, coat with the breadcrumb's mixture.

4. Arrange the eggplant slices in Air Fryer Basket inside the Instant Pot. Put on the Instant Air Fryer lid and cook on Air Fry mode for 8 minutes at 390 degrees F. Once done, remove the lid and serve warm.

Nutrition: calories: 146 Protein: 6.3g Carbs: 18.8g Fat: 4.5g

47. Roasted Pecans

Preparation time: 5 minutes.

Cooking Time: 9 minutes.

Servings: 2

Ingredients:

- 1½ cups of raw Pecans

- A pinch of Salt

- Nonstick cooking spray

Directions:

1. Spread the pecans in the Instant Pot and toss them with salt and cooking oil. Put on the Instant Air Fryer lid and cook on Air Fry mode for 9 minutes at 320 degrees F.

2. Once done, remove the lid and serve warm.

Nutrition: calories: 207 Protein: 9.4g Carbs: 5.9g Fat: 18g

48. Crispy Broccoli Poppers

Preparation time: 5 minutes.

Cooking Time: 10 minutes. **Servings:** 4

Ingredients:

- 2 tablespoons plain yogurt

- ½ teaspoon red chili powder

- ¼ teaspoon ground cumin

- ¼ teaspoon ground turmeric

- Salt, to taste

- 1 lb. broccoli, cut into small florets

- 2 tablespoons chickpea flour

Directions:

1. In a bowl, mix together the yogurt, and spices. Add the broccoli and coat with marinade generously. Refrigerate for about 20 minutes. Arrange the broccoli florets in Air Fryer Basket inside the Instant Pot. Put on the Instant Air Fryer lid and cook on Air Fry mode for 10 minutes at 390 degrees F.

2. Once done, remove the lid and serve warm.

Nutrition: calories: 202 Protein: 5.3g Carbs: 11.2g Fat: 16.5g

49.   Potato Cheese Croquettes

Preparation time: 15 minutes.

Cooking Time: 9 minutes.

Servings: 6

Ingredients:

- 2 medium Russet potatoes, peeled and cubed

- 2 tablespoons all-purpose flour

- ½ cup Parmesan cheese, grated

- 1 egg yolk

- 2 tablespoons chives, minced

- Pinch of ground nutmeg

- Salt and black pepper, as needed

- 2 eggs

- ½ cup breadcrumbs

- 2 tablespoons vegetable oil

Directions:

1. In a pot of boiling water, add the potatoes and cook for about 15 minutes. Drain the potatoes well and transfer into a large bowl.

2. With a potato masher, mash the potatoes and set aside to cool completely. In the bowl of mashed potatoes, add the flour, Parmesan

cheese, egg yolk, chives, nutmeg, salt, and black pepper then mix until well combined.

3. Make small equalized balls from the mixture. Now, roll each ball into a cylinder shape. In a shallow dish, crack the eggs and beat well.

4. In another container, mix together the breadcrumbs and oil. Dip the croquettes in the egg mixture and then coat with the breadcrumb's mixture.

5. Arrange the croquettes in Air Fryer Basket inside the Instant Pot.

6. Put on the Instant Air Fryer lid and cook on Air Fry mode for 9 minutes at 390 degrees F. Once done, remove the lid and serve warm.

Nutrition: calories: 172 Protein: 2.1g Carbs: 18.6g Fat: 10.7g

50. Breaded Chicken Nuggets

Preparation time: 10 minutes.

Cooking Time: 10 minutes.

Servings: 6

Ingredients:

- 2 large chicken breasts, cut into 1inch cubes

- 1 cup breadcrumbs

- 1/3 tablespoon Parmesan cheese, shredded

- 1 teaspoon onion powder

- ¼ teaspoon smoked paprika

- Salt and ground black pepper, as required

Directions:

1. In a large resalable bag, add all the Ingredients. Seal the bag and shake well to coat completely.

2. Arrange the nuggets in Air Fryer Basket inside the Instant Pot. Put on the Instant Air Fryer lid and cook on Air Fry mode for 10 minutes at 400 degrees F. Once done, remove the lid and serve warm.

Nutrition: calories: 151 Protein: 1.9g Carbs: 6.9g Fat: 8.6g

30 DAYS MEAL PLAN

Days	Breakfast	Snacks	Dinner
1	Sausage and Egg Breakfast Burrito	Eggplant Mix	Roasted Salmon with Lemon and Rosemary
2	Eggs in Avocado	Garlic Kale	Air Fried Meatballs with Parsley
3	French Toast Sticks	Herbed Tomatoes	Succulent Flank Steak
4	Home-Fried Potatoes	Coriander Potatoes	Chili Roasted Eggplant Soba
5	Homemade Cherry Breakfast Tarts	Tomatoes and Green beans	Quinoa and Spinach Cakes
6	Sausage and Cream Cheese Biscuits	Buttery Artichokes	Air Fried Cajun Shrimp
7	Fried Chicken and Waffles	Ginger Mushrooms	Air Fried Squid Rings
8	Cheesy Tater Tot Breakfast Bake	Masala Potatoes	Marinated Portobello Mushroom
9	Breakfast Scramble Casserole	Mixed Veggie Chips	Air Fried Meatloaf
10	Homemade Cherry Breakfast Tarts	Pear and Apple Chips	Fettuccini with Roasted Vegetables in Tomato Sauce
11	Mozzarella Tots	Banana and Cocoa Chips	Herbed Parmesan Turkey Meatballs
12	Chicken Balls	Roasted Chickpeas	Teriyaki Glazed Salmon and Vegetable Roast

13	Tofu Egg Scramble	Zucchini Chips	Sirloin with Garlic and Thyme
14	Flax & Hemp Porridge	Ranch Garlic Pretzels	Herbed Parmesan Turkey Meatballs
15	Creamy Bacon Eggs	Yellow Squash and Cream Cheese Fritters	Yogurt Garlic Chicken
16	Cheddar Bacon Hash	Air Fry Cheesy Taco Hot dogs	Lemony Parmesan Salmon
17	Cheddar Soufflé with Herbs	Crispy French Toast Sticks	Easiest Tuna Cobbler Ever
18	Bacon Butter Biscuits	Buttered Corn Cob	Deliciously Homemade Pork Buns
19	Keto Parmesan Frittata	Roasted Cashews	Mouthwatering Tuna Melts
20	Chicken Liver Pate	Panko Zucchini Fries	Bacon Wings
21	Coconut Pancake Hash	Rosemary Turnip Chips	Pepper Pesto Lamb
22	Beef Slices	Rosemary Carrot Fries	Tuna Spinach Casserole
23	Flax & Chia Porridge	Butternut Squash Fries	Greek Style Mini Burger Pies
24	Paprika Eggs with Bacon	Breaded Pickle Fries	Family Fun Pizza
25	Quiche Muffin Cups	Buttered Corn Cob	Crispy Hot Sauce Chicken
26	Easy Scotch Eggs	Polenta Bars	Herbed Parmesan Turkey Meatballs
27	Strawberry Toast	Eggplant Crisps	Sweet Potatoes & Creamy Crisp Chicken
28	Cinnamon Sweet-Potato Chips	Roasted Pecans	Mushroom & Chicken Noodles with Glasswort and Sesame

29	Quiche Muffin Cups	Crispy Broccoli Poppers	Prawn Chicken Drumettes
30	Vegetable and Ham Omelet	Potato Cheese Croquettes	Asian Popcorn Chicken

CONCLUSION

The concept of an air fryer is to fry food items in the air instead of oil. This revolutionary kitchen appliance uses superheated air that circulates to cook the food. This way, you don't have to dunk your food in sizzling hot fat just to achieve that crunch.

Regarding structure, an air fryer almost looks like a large rice cooker but with a front door handle. It has a removable chunky tray that holds the food to the air fried. It has an integrated timer to allow you to pre-set cooking times, and an adjustable temperature control so you can pre-set the best cooking temperature.

Different models offer different features, such as digital displays, auto-power shut-off, but mostly they work the same and use the same technology.

The air fryers have gained a lot of popularity over the last years due to their many advantages. Cooking in an air fryer is such a great and fun experience and you should try it as soon as possible.

The air fryer is such an innovative appliance that allows you to cook some of the best, most succulent and rich meals for you, your family and friends.

The air fryer reduces the cooking time and the effort you spend in the kitchen.

Having an air fryer is a great option. You can enjoy a healthier meal and save a good part of the oil expense, all without giving up enjoyable, fried foods.

Get a copy of this amazing air fryer cooking guide and use it to make real feast using this great appliance.

Start this culinary journey right away and enjoy the benefits of cooking with the air fryer.

Keto Air Fryer

Cookbook 2021

Amazingly Delicious Low-Carb Recipes for the Busy People on Keto Diet

Nicole S. Rodriguez

© Copyright 2021 - All rights reserved.

INTRODUCTION

Air Fryers has quickly become a staple of the kitchen, providing a quick and efficient method of cooking. Requiring far less oil than traditional frying ways, air fryers is the best way to produce meals that are fast and healthy and that can be the foundation of a balanced keto lifestyle. Other than that, they can be a great way to help you incorporate healthier fats into your ketogenic diet.

In this book, you will find a selection of keto recipes that are easy to prepare and cook with a fryer.

So what is a Air fryer? At the most basic level, a fryer operates with the circulation of hot air around the food, ensuring a thorough and uniform cooking process, with temperatures and times adjusted accordingly. Similar to traditional fryers, food is placed in a cooking basket, but requires much less oil, making it a much healthier choice. The fryer also offers many cooking methods, all in a neat unit, such as roasting, baking or roasting.

Once you have grasped the basics of the fryer, you can consider possible accessories and additional accessories to best increase your cooking range.

People who follow the ketogenic diet limit the intake of carbohydrates to around 20 to 30 net grams daily or 5% of the daily diet. Net grams refer to the number of carbohydrates that remain after subtracting the grams of dietary fiber. Since the carbohydrate intake is limited, dieters are encouraged to consume more fat and protein in amounts of 80% and 20%; respectively.

It is important to note that ketogenic diet is entirely different from the other low-carb diets that encourage protein loading. Protein is not as important as fat is in the ketogenic diet. The reason is that the presence of a higher amount of protein pushes the body to the process called gluconeogenesis wherein protein is converted into glucose. If this happens, the body is not pushed to a state of ketosis. This is the reason why it is so crucial to consume more fat under the ketogenic diet than protein.

When we eat, the carbohydrates found in the food that we consume is converted into a simple sugar called glucose. Alongside converting carbs to glucose, the pancreas also manufactures insulin, which is a hormone responsible for pushing glucose into the cells to be used up as energy.

As glucose is used up as the main source of energy, the fats that you also consume from food is not utilized thus they are immediately stored in the liver and adipocytes (specialized fat cells). Moreover, if you consume too many carbohydrates, the glucose that is not used up is converted into glycogen and is stored in the liver and muscles as standby energy source. If not used up, it is processed and converted to fat and stored all over the body, thus you gain weight.

If you are new to your keto journey and you don't have kitchen skill, an air fryer is a great venture to help kick start your new culinary quest – and the recipes in this book provide a great starting point.

BREAKFAST

Mozzarella Tots

Preparation time: 12 minutes

Cooking time: 3 minutes

Servings: 5

Ingredients:

- 8 oz. mozzarella balls
- 1 egg
- ½ cup coconut flakes
- ½ cup almond flour
- 1 teaspoon thyme
- 1 teaspoon ground black pepper
- 1 teaspoon paprika

Directions:

1. Crack the egg in a bowl and whisk.
2. Combine the coconut flour with the thyme, ground black pepper, and paprika. Stir carefully.
3. Sprinkle Mozzarella balls with the coconut flakes.
4. Transfer the balls to the whisked egg mixture.
5. Coat in the almond flour mixture.

6. Put Mozzarella balls in the freezer for 5 minutes.

7. Meanwhile, preheat the air fryer to 400 F.

8. Put the frozen cheese balls in the preheated air fryer and cook them for 3 minutes.

9. Remove the cheese tots from the air fryer basket and chill them for 2 minutes.

Nutrition: calories 166, fat 12.8, fiber 1.4, carbs 2.8, protein 9.5

Chicken Balls

Preparation time: 10 minutes

Cooking time: 8 minutes

Servings: 5

Ingredients:

- 8 oz. ground chicken

- 1 egg white

- 1 tablespoon dried parsley

- ½ teaspoon salt

- ½ teaspoon ground black pepper

- 2 tablespoon almond flour

- 1 tablespoon olive oil

- 1 teaspoon paprika

Directions:

1. Whisk the egg white and combine it with the ground chicken.

2. Sprinkle the chicken mixture with the dried parsley and salt.

3. Add ground black pepper and paprika.

4. Stir carefully using a spoon.

5. Using wet hands, make small balls from the ground chicken mixture.

6. Sprinkle each sausage ball with the almond flour.

7. Preheat the air fryer to 380 F.

8. Grease the air fryer basket tray with olive oil and place the sausage balls inside.

9. Cook for 8 minutes.

10. Turn halfway to crisp each side.
11. Serve hot.

Nutrition: calories 180, fat 11.8, fiber 1.5, carbs 2.9, protein 16.3

Tofu Egg Scramble

Preparation time: 15 minutes

Cooking time: 20 minutes

Servings: 5

Ingredients:

- 10 oz tofu cheese

- 2 eggs

- 1 teaspoon chives

- 1 tablespoon apple cider vinegar

- ½ teaspoon salt

- 1 teaspoon ground white pepper

- ¼ teaspoon ground coriander

Directions:

1. Shred the tofu and sprinkle it with the apple cider vinegar, salt, ground white pepper, and ground coriander.

2. Mix and leave for 10 minutes to marinade.

3. Meanwhile, preheat the air fryer to 370 F.

4. Transfer the marinated tofu to the air fryer basket tray and cook for 13 minutes.

5. Meanwhile, crack the eggs in a bowl and whisk them.

6. When the tofu has cooked, pour the egg mixture in the shredded tofu cheese and stir with a spatula.

7. When the eggs start to firm place the air fryer basket tray in the air fryer and cook the dish for 7 minutes more.

8. Remove the cooked meal from the air fryer basket tray and serve.

Nutrition: calories 109, fat 6.7, fiber 1.4, carbs 2.9, protein 11.2

Flax & Hemp Porridge

Preparation time: 10 minutes

Cooking time: 15 minutes

Servings: 3

Ingredients:

- 2 tablespoon flax seeds
- 4 tablespoon hemp seeds
- 1 tablespoon butter
- ¼ teaspoon salt
- 1 teaspoon stevia
- 7 tablespoon almond milk
- ½ teaspoon ground ginger

Directions:

1. Place the flax seeds and hemp seeds in the air fryer basket.
2. Sprinkle the seeds with salt and ground ginger.
3. Combine the almond milk and stevia together. Stir the liquid and pour it into the seed mixture.
4. Add butter.
5. Preheat the air fryer to 370 F and cook the hemp seed porridge for 15 minutes.
6. Stir carefully after 10 minutes of cooking.
7. Remove the hem porridge from the air fryer basket tray and chill it for 3 minutes.
8. Transfer the porridge into serving bowls.

Nutrition: calories 196, fat 18.2, fiber 2.4, carbs 4.2, protein 5.1

Creamy Bacon Eggs

Preparation time: 10 minutes

Cooking time: 10 minutes

Servings: 4

Ingredients:

- 6 oz. bacon

- 4 eggs

- 5 tablespoon heavy cream

- 1 tablespoon butter

- 1 teaspoon paprika

- ½ teaspoon nutmeg

- 1 teaspoon salt

- 1 teaspoon ground black pepper

Directions:

1. Chop the bacon into small pieces and sprinkle it with salt.
2. Mix to combine and put in the air fryer basket.
3. Preheat the air fryer to 360 F and cook the bacon for 5 minutes.
4. Meanwhile, crack the eggs in a bowl and whisk them using a hand whisker.
5. Sprinkle the egg mixture with paprika, nutmeg, and ground black pepper.
6. Whisk egg mixture gently.
7. Toss the butter into the bacon and pour the egg mixture.
8. Add the heavy cream and cook for 2 minutes.
9. Stir the mixture with a spatula until you get scrambled eggs and cook for 3 minutes more.
10. Transfer onto serving plates.

Nutrition: calories 387, fat 32.1, fiber 0.4, carbs 2.3, protein 21.9

Cheddar Bacon Hash

Preparation time: 8 minutes

Cooking time: 8 minutes

Servings: 4

Ingredients:

- 1 zucchini

- 7 oz. bacon, cooked

- 4 oz. Cheddar cheese

- 2 tablespoon butter

- 1 teaspoon salt

- 1 teaspoon ground black pepper

- 1 teaspoon paprika

- 1 teaspoon cilantro

- 1 teaspoon ground thyme

Directions:

1. Chop the zucchini into the small cubes and sprinkle it with salt, ground black pepper, paprika, cilantro, and ground thyme.

2. Preheat the air fryer to 400 F and toss the butter into the air fryer basket tray.

3. Melt it and add the zucchini cubes.

4. Cook the zucchini for 5 minutes.

5. Meanwhile, shred Cheddar cheese.

6. Shake the zucchini cubes carefully and add the cooked bacon.

7. Sprinkle the zucchini mixture with the shredded cheese and cook it for 3 minutes more.

8. Transfer the breakfast hash in the serving bowls and stir.

Nutrition: calories 445, fat 36.1, fiber 1, carbs 3.5, protein 26.3

Cheddar Soufflé with Herbs

Preparation time: 10 minutes

Cooking time: 8 minutes

Servings: 4

Ingredients:

- 5 oz. Cheddar cheese, shredded
- 3 eggs
- 4 tablespoon heavy cream
- 1 tablespoon chives
- 1 tablespoon dill
- 1 teaspoon parsley
- ½ teaspoon ground thyme

Directions:

1. Crack the eggs into a bowl and whisk them carefully.
2. Add the heavy cream and whisk it for 10 seconds more.
3. Add the chives, dill, parsley, and ground thyme.
4. Sprinkle the egg mixture with the shredded cheese and stir it.
5. Transfer the egg mixture into 4 ramekins and place the ramekins in the air fryer basket.
6. Preheat the air fryer to 390 F and cook the soufflé for 8 minutes.
7. Once cooked, chill well.

Nutrition: calories 244, fat 20.6, fiber 0.2, carbs 1.7, protein 13.5

Bacon Butter Biscuits

Preparation time: 15 minutes

Cooking time: 10 minutes

Servings: 6

Ingredients:

- 1 egg

- 4 oz. bacon, cooked

- 1 cup almond flour

- ½ teaspoon baking soda

- 1 tablespoon apple cider vinegar

- 3 tablespoon butter

- 4 tablespoon heavy cream

- 1 teaspoon dried oregano

Directions:

1. Crack the egg in a bowl and whisk it.
2. Chop the cooked bacon and add it into the whisked egg.
3. Sprinkle the mixture with baking soda and apple cider vinegar.
4. Add the heavy cream and dried oregano. Stir.
5. Add butter and almond flour.
6. Mix well with a hand mixer.
7. When you get a smooth and liquid batter – the dough is cooked.
8. Preheat the air fryer to 400 F.
9. Pour the batter dough into muffin molds.
10. When the air fryer is heated put the muffin molds in the air fryer basket and cook them for 10 minutes.
11. Chill the muffins to room temperature.

Nutrition: calories 226, fat 20.5, fiber 0.6, carbs 1.8, protein 9.2

Keto Parmesan Frittata

Preparation time: 10 minutes

Cooking time: 15 minutes

Servings: 6

Ingredients:

- 6 eggs
- 1/3 cup heavy cream
- 1 tomato
- 5 oz chive stems
- 1 tablespoon butter
- 1 teaspoon salt
- 1 tablespoon dried oregano
- 6 oz. Parmesan
- 1 teaspoon chili pepper

Directions:

1. Crack the eggs into the air fryer basket tray and whisk them with a hand whisker.

2. Chop the tomato and dice the chives.

3. Add the vegetables to the egg mixture.

4. Pour the heavy cream.

5. Sprinkle the liquid mixture with the butter, salt, dried oregano, and chili pepper.

6. Shred Parmesan cheese and add it to the mixture too.

7. Sprinkle the mixture with a silicone spatula.

8. Preheat the air fryer to 375 F and cook the frittata for 15 minutes.

Nutrition: calories 202, fat 15, fiber 0.7, carbs 3.4, protein 15.1

Chicken Liver Pate

Preparation time: 10 minutes

Cooking time: 10 minutes

Servings: 7

Ingredients:

- 1-pound chicken liver
- 1 teaspoon salt
- 4 tablespoon butter
- 1 cup water
- 1 teaspoon ground black pepper
- 5 oz chive stems
- ½ teaspoon dried cilantro

Directions:

1. Chop the chicken liver roughly and place it in the air fryer basket tray.
2. Dice the chives.
3. Pour the water in the air fryer basket tray and add the diced chives.
4. Preheat the air fryer to 360 F and cook the chicken liver for 10 minutes.
5. Once cooked, strain the chicken liver mixture to discard the liquid.
6. Transfer the chicken liver into a blender.
7. Add the butter, ground black pepper, and dried cilantro.

8. Blend the mixture till you get the pate texture.

9. Transfer the liver pate to a bowl and serve it immediately or keep in the fridge.

Nutrition: calories 173, fat 10.8, fiber 0.4, carbs 2.2, protein 16.1

VEGETABLE RECIPES

Crisp & Crunchy Asparagus

Preparation Time: 10 minutes

Cooking Time: 10 minutes

Servings: 4

Ingredients:

- 1 lb asparagus, trim ends & cut in half
- 1 tablespoon vinegar
- 2 tablespoon coconut aminos
- 1 tablespoon butter, melted
- 1 tablespoon olive oil
- 1/2 teaspoon sea salt

Directions:

1. In a bowl, toss asparagus with olive oil and salt.
2. Place the cooking tray in the air fryer basket.
3. Select Air Fry mode.
4. Set time to 10 minutes and temperature 400 F then press START.
5. The air fryer display will prompt you to ADD FOOD once the temperature is reached then add asparagus in the air fryer basket.
6. Meanwhile, for the sauce in a bowl, mix together coconut aminos, melted butter, and vinegar.
7. Pour sauce over hot asparagus and serve.

Nutrition: Calories 86 Fat 6.5 g Carbohydrates 5.9 g Sugar 2.2 g Protein 2.5 g Cholesterol 8 mg

Balsamic Brussels Sprouts

Preparation Time: 10 minutes

Cooking Time: 20 minutes

Servings: 4

Ingredients:

- 1 lb brussels sprouts, cut in half
- 1 small onion, sliced
- 3 bacon slices, cut into pieces
- 1 teaspoon garlic powder
- 2 tablespoon fresh lemon juice
- 2 tablespoon balsamic vinegar
- 3 tablespoon olive oil
- 1/2 teaspoon sea salt

Directions:

1. In a small bowl, whisk together balsamic vinegar, olive oil, lemon juice, garlic powder, and salt.
2. Toss brussels sprouts with 3 tablespoons of the balsamic vinegar mixture.
3. Place the cooking tray in the air fryer basket.
4. Select Air Fry mode.
5. Set time to 20 minutes and temperature 370 F then press START.
6. The air fryer display will prompt you to ADD FOOD once the temperature is reached then add brussels sprouts in the air fryer basket.
7. After 10 minutes toss Brussels sprouts and top with bacon and onion and air fry for 10 minutes more.
8. Drizzle remaining balsamic vinegar mixture over brussels sprouts and serve.

Nutrition: Calories 229 Fat 16.9 g Carbohydrates 12.9 g Sugar 3.6 g Protein 9.5 g Cholesterol 16 mg

Healthy Roasted Vegetables

Preparation Time: 10 minutes

Cooking Time: 14 minutes

Servings: 4

Ingredients:

- 8 oz asparagus, cut the ends
- 8 oz mushrooms, halved
- 1 zucchini, sliced
- 6 oz grape tomatoes
- 1/2 teaspoon pepper
- 1 tablespoon Dijon mustard
- 1 tablespoon soy sauce
- 1/4 cup balsamic vinegar
- 4 tablespoon olive oil

Directions:

1. In a large bowl, mix together olive oil, vinegar, soy sauce, Dijon mustard, and pepper.
2. Add asparagus, tomatoes, zucchini, and mushrooms into the bowl and toss until well coated.
3. Place vegetables in the refrigerator for 30 minutes.
4. Place the cooking tray in the air fryer basket.
5. Select Air Fry mode.
6. Set time to 14 minutes and temperature 400 F then press START.
7. The air fryer display will prompt you to ADD FOOD once the temperature is reached then add marinated vegetables in the air fryer basket. Stir vegetables halfway through.
8. Serve and enjoy.

Nutrition: Calories 168 Fat 14.6 g Carbohydrates 8.2 g Sugar 4.2 g Protein 4.4 g Cholesterol 0 mg

Parmesan Zucchini Noodles

Preparation Time: 10 minutes

Cooking Time: 10 minutes

Servings: 2

Ingredients:

- 4 cups zucchini noodles
- 1/2 cup parmesan cheese, grated
- 2 tablespoon mayonnaise

Directions:

1. Add zucchini noodles into the microwave-safe bowl and microwave for 3 minutes. Pat dry zucchini noodles with a paper towel.
2. In a mixing bowl, toss zucchini noodles with parmesan cheese and mayonnaise.
3. Place the cooking tray in the air fryer basket. Line air fryer basket with parchment paper.
4. Select Air Fry mode.
5. Set time to 10 minutes and temperature 400 F then press START.
6. The air fryer display will prompt you to ADD FOOD once the temperature is reached then add zucchini noodles onto the parchment paper in the air fryer basket. Stir zucchini noodles halfway through.
7. Serve and enjoy.

Nutrition: Calories 261 Fat 17.6 g Carbohydrates 8.9 g Sugar 2.6 g Protein 20.1 g Cholesterol 46 mg

Rosemary Basil Mushrooms

Preparation Time: 10 minutes

Cooking Time: 14 minutes

Servings: 4

Ingredients:

- 1 lb mushrooms
- 1/2 tablespoon vinegar
- 1/2 teaspoon ground coriander
- 1 teaspoon rosemary, chopped
- 1 tablespoon basil, minced
- 1 garlic clove, minced
- Pepper
- Salt

Directions:

1. Add all ingredients into the large bowl and toss well.
2. Select Air Fry mode.
3. Set time to 14 minutes and temperature 350 F then press START.
4. The air fryer display will prompt you to ADD FOOD once the temperature is reached then add mushrooms in the air fryer basket.
5. Serve and enjoy.

Nutrition: Calories 27 Fat 0.4 g Carbohydrates 4.2 g Sugar 2 g Protein 3.6 g Cholesterol 0 mg

Baked Brussels Sprouts

Preparation Time: 10 minutes

Cooking Time: 35 minutes

Servings: 6

Ingredients:

- 2 cups Brussels sprouts, halved
- 1/4 teaspoon garlic powder
- 1/4 cup olive oil
- 1/2 teaspoon cayenne pepper
- 1/4 teaspoon salt

Directions:

1. Add all ingredients into the large bowl and toss well.
2. Select Bake mode.
3. Set time to 35 minutes and temperature 400 F then press START.
4. The air fryer display will prompt you to ADD FOOD once the temperature is reached then add brussels sprouts in the air fryer basket.
5. Serve and enjoy.

Nutrition: Calories 86 Fat 8.5 g Carbohydrates 2.8 g Sugar 0.7 g Protein 1 g Cholesterol 0 mg

Old Bay Cauliflower Florets

Preparation Time: 10 minutes

Cooking Time: 15 minutes

Servings: 4

Ingredients:

- 1 medium cauliflower head, cut into florets
- 1/2 teaspoon old bay seasoning
- 1/4 teaspoon paprika
- 1 tablespoon garlic, minced
- 3 tablespoon olive oil
- Pepper
- Salt

Directions:

1. In a large bowl, toss cauliflower with remaining ingredients.
2. Select Air Fry mode.
3. Set time to 15 minutes and temperature 400 F then press START.
4. The air fryer display will prompt you to ADD FOOD once the temperature is reached then add cauliflower florets in the air fryer basket.
5. Serve and enjoy.

Nutrition: Calories 130 Fat 10.7 g Carbohydrates 8.4 g Sugar 3.5 g Protein 3 g Cholesterol 0 mg

Rosemary Mushrooms

Preparation Time: 10 minutes

Cooking Time: 14 minutes

Servings: 4

Ingredients:

- 1 lb mushroom caps
- 1/2 teaspoon ground coriander
- 1 teaspoon rosemary, chopped
- 1/2 teaspoon garlic powder
- Pepper
- Salt

Directions:

1. Add all ingredients into the mixing bowl and toss well.
2. Select Air Fry mode.
3. Set time to 14 minutes and temperature 350 F then press START.
4. The air fryer display will prompt you to ADD FOOD once the temperature is reached then add mushrooms in the air fryer basket.
5. Serve and enjoy.

Nutrition: Calories 27 Fat 0.4 g Carbohydrates 4.2 g Sugar 2 g Protein 3.6 g Cholesterol 0 mg

Air Fry Bell Peppers

Preparation Time: 10 minutes

Cooking Time: 8 minutes

Servings: 3

Ingredients:

- 1 cup red bell peppers, cut into chunks
- 1 cup green bell peppers, cut into chunks
- 1 cup yellow bell peppers, cut into chunks
- 1 teaspoon olive oil
- 1/4 teaspoon garlic powder
- Pepper
- Salt

Directions:

1. Add all ingredients into the large bowl and toss well.
2. Select Air Fry mode.
3. Set time to 8 minutes and temperature 360 F then press START.
4. The air fryer display will prompt you to ADD FOOD once the temperature is reached then add bell peppers in the air fryer basket. Stir halfway through.
5. Serve and enjoy.

Nutrition: Calories 52 Fat 1.9 g Carbohydrates 9.2 g Sugar 6.1 g Protein 1.2 g Cholesterol 0 mg

Air Fry Baby Carrots

Preparation Time: 10 minutes

Cooking Time: 12 minutes

Servings: 4

Ingredients:

- 3 cups baby carrots
- 1 tablespoon olive oil
- Pepper
- Salt

Directions:

1. Add carrots, oil, pepper, and salt into the mixing bowl and toss well.
2. Select Bake mode.
3. Set time to 12 minutes and temperature 390 F then press START.
4. The air fryer display will prompt you to ADD FOOD once the temperature is reached then add baby carrots in the air fryer basket. Stir halfway through.
5. Serve and enjoy.

Nutrition: Calories 52 Fat 3.6 g Carbohydrates 5.3 g Sugar 3 g Protein 0.4 g Cholesterol 0 mg

SEAFOOD RECIPES

Old Bay Shrimp

Preparation Time: 10 minutes

Cooking Time: 10 minutes

Servings: 4

Ingredients:

- 12 oz shrimp, peeled
- 3/25 oz pork rind, crushed
- 1 1/2 teaspoon old bay seasoning
- 1/4 cup mayonnaise

Directions:

1. In a shallow bowl, mix together crushed pork rind and old bay seasoning.
2. Add shrimp and mayonnaise into the mixing bowl and toss well.
3. Place the cooking tray in the air fryer basket.
4. Select Air Fry mode.
5. Set time to 10 minutes and temperature 380 F then press START.
6. The air fryer display will prompt you to ADD FOOD once the temperature is reached then coat shrimp with crushed pork rind and place in the air fryer basket.
7. Serve and enjoy.

Nutrition: Calories 163 Fat 6.7 g Carbohydrates 4.8 g Sugar 0.9 g Protein 20.1 g Cholesterol 184 mg

Crunchy Fish Sticks

Preparation Time: 10 minutes

Cooking Time: 15 minutes

Servings: 5

Ingredients:

- 12 oz tilapia loins, cut into fish sticks
- 1/2 cup parmesan cheese, grated
- 3.25 oz pork rind, crushed
- 1 teaspoon paprika
- 1 teaspoon garlic powder
- 1/4 cup mayonnaise

Directions:

1. In a shallow bowl, mix together parmesan cheese, crushed pork rind, paprika, and garlic powder.
2. Add fish pieces and mayonnaise into the mixing bowl and mix well.
3. Place the cooking tray in the air fryer basket.
4. Select Air Fry mode.
5. Set time to 15 minutes and temperature 380 F then press START.
6. The air fryer display will prompt you to ADD FOOD once the temperature is reached then coat fish pieces with parmesan mixture and place in the air fryer basket.
7. Serve and enjoy.

Nutrition: Calories 295 Fat 16.8 g Carbohydrates 4.3 g Sugar 0.9 g Protein 33.4 g Cholesterol 61 mg

Garlic Butter Fish Fillets

Preparation Time: 10 minutes

Cooking Time: 10 minutes

Servings: 2

Ingredients:

- 2 salmon fillets
- 1/4 teaspoon dried parsley
- 1 teaspoon garlic, minced
- 2 tablespoon butter, melted
- Pepper
- Salt

Directions:

1. In a small bowl, mix together melted butter, garlic, and parsley.
2. Season fish fillets with pepper and salt and brush with melted butter mixture.
3. Place the cooking tray in the air fryer basket.
4. Select Air Fry mode.
5. Set time to 10 minutes and temperature 360 F then press START.
6. The air fryer display will prompt you to ADD FOOD once the temperature is reached then place fish fillets skin side down in the air fryer basket.
7. Serve and enjoy.

Nutrition: Calories 340 Fat 22.5 g Carbohydrates 0.5 g Sugar 0 g Protein 34.8 g Cholesterol 109 mg

Parmesan Shrimp

Preparation Time: 10 minutes

Cooking Time: 12 minutes

Servings: 4

Ingredients:

- 1 lb shrimp, peeled & deveined
- 2 tablespoon parsley, minced
- 2 tablespoon parmesan cheese, grated
- 1/8 teaspoon garlic powder
- 2 tablespoon olive oil
- 1/2 teaspoon pepper
- 1/2 teaspoon salt

Directions:

1. In a mixing bowl, toss shrimp with olive oil. Add remaining ingredients and toss until shrimp is well coated.
2. Place the cooking tray in the air fryer basket.
3. Select Air Fry mode.
4. Set time to 12 minutes and temperature 400 F then press START.
5. The air fryer display will prompt you to ADD FOOD once the temperature is reached then add shrimp in the air fryer basket.
6. Stir shrimp halfway through.
7. Serve and enjoy.

Nutrition: Calories 205 Fat 9.5 g Carbohydrates 2.2 g Sugar 0 g Protein 26.8 g Cholesterol 241 mg

Flavorful Tuna Steaks

Preparation Time: 10 minutes

Cooking Time: 4 minutes

Servings: 2

Ingredients:

- 12 tuna steaks, skinless and boneless
- 1/2 teaspoon rice vinegar
- 1 teaspoon sesame oil
- 1 teaspoon ginger, grated
- 4 tablespoon soy sauce

Directions:

1. Add tuna steaks and remaining ingredients in the zip-lock bag. Seal bag and place in the refrigerator for 30 minutes.
2. Select Air Fry mode.
3. Set time to 4 minutes and temperature 380 F then press START.
4. The air fryer display will prompt you to ADD FOOD once the temperature is reached then place marinated tuna steaks in the air fryer basket.
5. Serve and enjoy.

Nutrition: Calories 980 Fat 34.4 g Carbohydrates 3.1 g Sugar 0.6 g Protein 154.7 g Cholesterol 250 mg

Baked Tilapia

Preparation Time: 10 minutes

Cooking Time: 15 minutes

Servings: 6

Ingredients:

- 6 tilapia fillets
- 1/2 cup Asiago cheese, grated
- 1/4 teaspoon basil
- 1/4 teaspoon thyme
- 1/4 teaspoon onion powder
- 1 teaspoon garlic, minced
- 1/2 cup mayonnaise
- 1/8 teaspoon pepper
- 1/4 teaspoon salt

Directions:

1. In a small bowl, mix together the grated cheese, basil, thyme, onion powder, garlic, mayonnaise, pepper, and salt.
2. Place the cooking tray in the air fryer basket. Line air fryer basket with parchment paper.
3. Select Bake mode.
4. Set time to 15 minutes and temperature 350 F then press START.
5. The air fryer display will prompt you to ADD FOOD once the temperature is reached then place fish fillets in the air fryer basket and spread cheese mixture on top of each fish fillet.
6. Serve and enjoy.

Nutrition: Calories 287 Fat 13.7 g Carbohydrates 5 g Sugar 1.3 g Protein 36.7 g Cholesterol 105 mg

Baked Parmesan Tilapia

Preparation Time: 10 minutes

Cooking Time: 10 minutes

Servings: 4

Ingredients:

- 2 lbs tilapia
- 1/4 teaspoon paprika
- 1/4 teaspoon dried basil
- 2 garlic cloves, minced
- 1 teaspoon dried parsley
- 1 tablespoon butter, softened
- 2 tablespoon fresh lemon juice
- 1/4 cup mayonnaise
- 1/2 cup parmesan cheese, grated
- 1/2 teaspoon salt

Directions:

1. In a small bowl, mix together parmesan cheese, mayonnaise, lemon juice, butter, parsley, garlic, basil, paprika, and salt.
2. Place the cooking tray in the air fryer basket. Line air fryer basket with parchment paper.
3. Select Bake mode.
4. Set time to 10 minutes and temperature 400 F then press START.
5. The air fryer display will prompt you to ADD FOOD once the temperature is reached then place fish fillets in the air fryer basket and spread the parmesan mixture on top of each fish fillet.
6. Serve and enjoy.

Nutrition: Calories 368 Fat 16.2 g Carbohydrates 5.3 g Sugar 1.1 g Protein 51.9 g Cholesterol 143 mg

Pecan Crusted Fish Fillets

Preparation Time: 10 minutes

Cooking Time: 17 minutes

Servings: 2

Ingredients:

- 2 halibut fillets
- 1/2 lemon juice
- 1 teaspoon garlic, minced
- 1/4 cup parmesan cheese, grated
- 1/4 cup pecans
- 2 tablespoon butter
- Pepper
- Salt

Directions:

1. Add pecans, lemon juice, garlic, parmesan cheese, and butter into the food processor and process until completely blended.
2. Place the cooking tray in the air fryer basket. Line air fryer basket with parchment paper.
3. Select Bake mode.
4. Set time to 5 minutes and temperature 400 F then press START.
5. The air fryer display will prompt you to ADD FOOD once the temperature is reached then season fish fillets with pepper and salt and place in the air fryer basket.
6. Spread pecan mixture on top of fish fillets and bake for 12 minutes more.
7. Serve and enjoy.

Nutrition: Calories 606 Fat 33.5 g Carbohydrates 3.6 g Sugar 0.7 g Protein 71.6 g Cholesterol 144 mg

Bagel Crust Fish Fillets

Preparation Time: 10 minutes

Cooking Time: 10 minutes

Servings: 4

Ingredients:

- 4 white fish fillets
- 1 tablespoon mayonnaise
- 1 teaspoon lemon pepper seasoning
- 2 tablespoon almond flour
- 1/4 cup bagel seasoning

Directions:

1. In a small bowl, mix together bagel seasoning, almond flour, and lemon pepper seasoning.
2. Brush mayonnaise over fish fillets. Sprinkle seasoning mixture over fish fillets.
3. Place the cooking tray in the air fryer basket. Line air fryer basket with parchment paper.
4. Select Bake mode.
5. Set time to 10 minutes and temperature 400 F then press START.
6. The air fryer display will prompt you to ADD FOOD once the temperature is reached then place fish fillets in the air fryer basket.
7. Serve and enjoy.

Nutrition: Calories 375 Fat 2.5 g Carbohydrates 7.2 g Sugar 1 g Protein 41.3 g Cholesterol 120 mg

Easy Air Fryer Scallops

Preparation Time: 10 minutes

Cooking Time: 4 minutes

Servings: 2

Ingredients:

- 8 scallops
- 1 tablespoon olive oil
- Pepper
- Salt

Directions:

1. Brush scallops with olive oil and season with pepper and salt.
2. Place the cooking tray in the air fryer basket.
3. Select Air Fry mode.
4. Set time to 2 minutes and temperature 390 F then press START.
5. The air fryer display will prompt you to ADD FOOD once the temperature is reached then add scallops in the air fryer basket.
6. Turn scallops and air fry for 2 minutes more.
7. Serve and enjoy.

Nutrition: Calories 166 Fat 7.9 g Carbohydrates 2.9 g Sugar 0 g Protein 20.2 g Cholesterol 40 mg

Pesto Scallops

Preparation Time: 10 minutes

Cooking Time: 7 minutes

Servings: 4

Ingredients:

- 1 lb sea scallops
- 2 teaspoon garlic, minced
- 3 tablespoon heavy cream
- 1/4 cup basil pesto
- 1 tablespoon olive oil
- 1/2 teaspoon pepper
- 1 teaspoon salt

Directions:

1. In a small pan, mix together oil, cream, garlic, pesto, pepper, and salt, and simmer for 2-3 minutes.
2. Select Air Fry mode.
3. Set time to 5 minutes and temperature 320 F then press START.
4. The air fryer display will prompt you to ADD FOOD once the temperature is reached then add scallops in the air fryer basket.
5. Turn scallops and after 3 minutes.
6. Transfer scallops into the mixing bowl.
7. Pour pesto sauce over scallops and serve.

Nutrition: Calories 172 Fat 8.6 g Carbohydrates 3.7 g Sugar 0 g Protein 19.4 g Cholesterol 53 mg

MEAT RECIPES

Pecan Dijon Pork Chops

Preparation Time: 10 minutes

Cooking Time: 12 minutes

Servings: 6

Ingredients:

- 1 egg
- 6 pork chops, boneless
- 2 garlic cloves, minced
- 1 tablespoon water
- 1 teaspoon Dijon mustard
- 1 teaspoon garlic powder
- 1 teaspoon onion powder
- 2 teaspoon Italian seasoning
- 1/3 cup arrowroot
- 1 cup pecans, finely chopped
- 1/4 teaspoon salt

Directions:

1. In a shallow bowl, whisk the egg with garlic, water, and Dijon mustard.

2. In a separate shallow bowl, mix together arrowroot, pecans, Italian seasoning, onion powder, garlic powder, and salt.

3. Dip pork chop in the egg mixture and coat with arrowroot mixture.

4. Place the cooking tray in the air fryer basket.

5. Select Air Fry mode.

6. Set time to 12 minutes and temperature 400 F then press START.

7. The air fryer display will prompt you to ADD FOOD once the temperature is reached then place coated pork chops in the air fryer basket.

8. Turn pork chops halfway through.

9. Serve and enjoy.

Nutrition: Calories 410 Fat 34.1 g Carbohydrates 4.8 g Sugar 1.1 g Protein 21.4 g Cholesterol 97 mg

Simple & Juicy Steak

Preparation Time: 10 minutes

Cooking Time: 13 minutes

Servings: 2

Ingredients:

- 12 oz ribeye steak

- 1 teaspoon steak seasoning

- 1 tablespoon olive oil

- Pepper

- Salt

Directions:

1. Coat steak with oil and season with steak seasoning, pepper, and salt.

2. Place the cooking tray in the air fryer basket.

3. Select Air Fry mode.

4. Set time to 13 minutes and temperature 400 F then press START.

5. The air fryer display will prompt you to ADD FOOD once the temperature is reached then place steak in the air fryer basket.

6. Serve and enjoy.

Nutrition: Calories 241 Fat 11.6 g Carbohydrates 0 g Sugar 0 g Protein 39.1 g Cholesterol 90 mg

Marinated Ribeye Steaks

Preparation Time: 10 minutes

Cooking Time: 12 minutes

Servings: 4

Ingredients:

- 2 large ribeye steaks, 1 1/2-inch thick

- 1 1/2 tablespoon Montreal steak seasoning

- 1/2 cup low-sodium soy sauce

- 1/4 cup olive oil

Directions:

1. Add soy sauce, oil, and Montreal steak seasoning in a large zip-lock bag.

2. Add steaks in a zip-lock bag. Seal bag shakes well and places in the refrigerator for 2 hours.

3. Place the cooking tray in the air fryer basket.

4. Select Air Fry mode.

5. Set time to 12 minutes and temperature 400 F then press START.

6. The air fryer display will prompt you to ADD FOOD once the temperature is reached then remove steaks from marinade and place in the air fryer basket.

7. Turn steaks halfway through.

8. Serve and enjoy.

Nutrition: Calories 186 Fat 14.1 g Carbohydrates 2 g Sugar 2 g Protein 15 g Cholesterol 3

Pork Chop Fries

Preparation Time: 10 minutes

Cooking Time: 15 minutes

Servings: 4

Ingredients:

- 1 lb pork chops, cut into fries

- 1/2 cup parmesan cheese, grated

- 3.5 oz pork rinds, crushed

- 1/2 cup ranch dressing

- Pepper

- Salt

Directions:

1. In a shallow dish, mix together crushed pork rinds, parmesan cheese, pepper, and salt.

2. Add pork chop pieces and ranch dressing into the zip-lock bag, seal bag, and shake well.

3. Remove pork chop pieces from zip-lock bag and coat with crushed pork rind mixture.

4. Place the cooking tray in the air fryer basket. Line air fryer basket with parchment paper.

5. Select Bake mode.

6. Set time to 15 minutes and temperature 400 F then press START.

7. The air fryer display will prompt you to ADD FOOD once the temperature is reached then place breaded pork chop fries in the air fryer basket.

8. Serve and enjoy.

Nutrition: Calories 608 Fat 43.4 g Carbohydrates 2.7 g Sugar 0.8 g Protein 51.2 g Cholesterol 154 mg

Pork Kebabs

Preparation Time: 10 minutes

Cooking Time: 15 minutes

Servings: 6

Ingredients:

- 2 lbs country-style pork ribs, cut into cubes

- 1/4 cup soy sauce

- 1/2 cup olive oil

- 1 tablespoon Italian seasoning

Directions:

1. Add soy sauce, oil, Italian seasoning, and pork cubes into the zip-lock bag, seal bag and place in the refrigerator for 4 hours.

2. Remove pork cubes from marinade and place the cubes on wooden skewers.

3. Place the cooking tray in the air fryer basket. Line air fryer basket with parchment paper.

4. Select Bake mode.

5. Set time to 15 minutes and temperature 380 F then press START.

6. The air fryer display will prompt you to ADD FOOD once the temperature is reached then place pork skewers in the air fryer basket.

7. Serve and enjoy.

Nutrition: Calories 438 Fat 34.9 g Carbohydrates 1.1 g Sugar 0.4 g Protein 30.1 g Cholesterol 115 mg

Feta Cheese Meatballs

Preparation Time: 10 minutes

Cooking Time: 12 minutes

Servings: 8

Ingredients:

- 2 lbs ground pork

- 2 eggs, lightly beaten

- 1/4 cup fresh parsley, chopped

- 1 tablespoon garlic, minced

- 1 onion, chopped

- 1 tablespoon Worcestershire sauce

- 1/2 cup feta cheese, crumbled

- 1/2 cup almond flour

- Pepper

- Salt

Directions:

1. Add all ingredients into the mixing bowl and mix until well combined.

2. Make small balls from the meat mixture.

3. Select Air Fry mode.

4. Set time to 12 minutes and temperature 400 F then press START.

5. The air fryer display will prompt you to ADD FOOD once the temperature is reached then place meatballs in the air fryer basket.

6. Serve and enjoy.

Nutrition: Calories 222 Fat 8 g Carbohydrates 3 g Sugar 1.5 gProtein 33.1 g Cholesterol 132 mg

Asian Meatballs

Preparation Time: 10 minutes

Cooking Time: 15 minutes

Servings: 4

Ingredients:

- 1 lb ground pork

- 1/2 lime juice

- 2 teaspoon curry paste

- 1 tablespoon Worcestershire sauce

- 1 tablespoon soy sauce

- 1 teaspoon garlic puree

- 1 teaspoon coriander

- 1 teaspoon Chinese spice

- 1 onion, chopped

- Pepper

- Salt

Directions:

1. Add ground meat and remaining ingredients into the large bowl and mix until well combined.

2. Make small meatballs from meat mixture.

3. Select Air Fry mode.

4. Set time to 15 minutes and temperature 350 F then press START.

5. The air fryer display will prompt you to ADD FOOD once the temperature is reached then place meatballs in the air fryer basket.

6. Serve and enjoy.

Nutrition: Calories 201 Fat 5.8 g Carbohydrates 4.9 g Sugar 2.1 g Protein 30.5 g Cholesterol 83 mg

Spicy Pork Patties

Preparation Time: 10 minutes

Cooking Time: 10 minutes

Servings: 2

Ingredients:

- 1/2 lb ground pork

- 1 tablespoon Cajun seasoning

- 1 egg, lightly beaten

- 1/2 cup almond flour

- Pepper

- Salt

Directions:

1. Add all ingredients into the large bowl and mix until well combined.

2. Make two equal shapes of patties from the meat mixture.

3. Select Air Fry mode.

4. Set time to 10 minutes and temperature 360 F then press START.

5. The air fryer display will prompt you to ADD FOOD once the temperature is reached then place patties in the air fryer basket.

6. Serve and enjoy.

Nutrition: Calories 234 Fat 9.7 g Carbohydrates 1.7 g Sugar 0.4 g Protein 34 g Cholesterol 165 mg

Herb Pork Chops

Preparation Time: 10 minutes

Cooking Time: 15 minutes

Servings: 4

Ingredients:

- 4 pork chops
- 2 teaspoon oregano
- 2 teaspoon thyme
- 2 teaspoon sage
- 1 teaspoon garlic powder
- 1 teaspoon paprika
- 1 teaspoon rosemary
- Pepper
- Salt

Directions:

1. Spray pork chops with cooking spray.
2. Mix together garlic powder, paprika, rosemary, oregano, thyme, sage, pepper, and salt and rub over pork chops.
3. Select Air Fry mode.
4. Set time to 15 minutes and temperature 360 F then press START.
5. The air fryer display will prompt you to ADD FOOD once the temperature is reached then place pork chops in the air fryer basket. Turn pork chops halfway through.

6. Serve and enjoy.

Nutrition: Calories 266 Fat 20.2 g Carbohydrates 2 g Sugar 0.3 g Protein 18.4 g Cholesterol 69 mg

SNACKS AND APPETIZERS

Parsley Shrimp Tails

Preparation time: 10 minutes

Cooking time: 14 minutes

Servings: 6

Ingredients:

- 1-pound shrimp tails
- 1 tablespoon olive oil
- 1 teaspoon dried dill
- ½ teaspoon dried parsley
- 2 tablespoon coconut flour
- ½ cup heavy cream
- 1 teaspoon chili flakes

Directions:

1. Peel the shrimp tails and sprinkle them with the dried dill and dried parsley.
2. Mix the shrimp tails carefully in a mixing bowl.
3. Combine the coconut flour, heavy cream, and chili flakes in a separate bowl and whisk until smooth.
4. Preheat the air fryer to 330 F.
5. Place the shrimp tails in the cream mix and stir.
6. Grease the air fryer rack and put the shrimp tails inside.
7. Cook the shrimp tails for 7 minutes.
8. Turn the shrimp.
9. Cook the shrimp tails for 7 minutes more.

Nutrition: calories 155, fat 7.6, fiber 1, carbs 3.2, protein 17.8

Calamari Almond Rings

Preparation time: 12 minutes

Cooking time: 8 minutes

Servings: 4

Ingredients:

- 1 cup almond flour

- 9 oz. calamari

- 1 egg

- ½ teaspoon lemon zest

- 1 teaspoon fresh lemon juice

- ½ teaspoon turmeric

- ¼ teaspoon salt

- ¼ teaspoon ground black pepper

Directions:

1. Wash and peel the calamari.
2. Slice the calamari into thick rings.
3. Crack the egg in a bowl and whisk it.
4. Add lemon zest, turmeric, salt, and ground black pepper to the bowl and mix.
5. Sprinkle the calamari rings with fresh lemon juice.
6. Place the calamari rings in the whisked egg and stir.
7. Leave the calamari rings in the egg mixture for 4 minutes.
8. Coat the calamari rings in the almond flour mixture well.
9. Preheat the air fryer to 360 F.
10. Transfer the calamari rings to the air fryer rack.
11. Cook the calamari rings for 8 minutes.

Nutrition: calories 190, fat 15.7, fiber 3.1, carbs 7, protein 8.7

Keto Beef Bombs

Preparation time: 15 minutes

Cooking time: 14 minutes

Servings: 7

Ingredients:

- 6 oz. ground chicken

- 6 oz. ground beef

- 6 oz. ground pork

- 2 oz chive stems

- 3 garlic cloves, minced

- 1 tablespoon dried parsley

- ½ teaspoon salt

- ½ teaspoon chili flakes

- 1 egg

- 1 tablespoon butter

Directions:

1. Put the ground chicken, ground beef, and ground pork in a mixing bowl.
2. Add the diced chives, minced garlic, dried parsley, salt, and chili flakes.
3. Crack the egg into the bowl with the ground meat.
4. Stir the meat mixture using your hands.
5. Melt butter and add it to the ground meat mixture.
6. Stir.
7. Leave the ground meat mixture for 5 minutes to rest.
8. Preheat the air fryer to 370 F.

9. Make small meatballs from the meat mixture and put them in the air fryer.
10. Cook the meatballs for 14 minutes.
11. Cool before serving.

Nutrition: calories 155, fat 6.5, fiber 0.2, carbs 1.3, protein 21.8

Paprika Mozzarella Balls

Preparation time: 10 minutes

Cooking time: 10 minutes

Servings: 6

Ingredients:

- 5 oz. bacon, sliced

- 10 oz. mozzarella

- ¼ teaspoon ground black pepper

- ¼ teaspoon paprika

Directions:

1. Sprinkle the sliced bacon with ground black pepper and paprika.
2. Wrap the mozzarella balls in the bacon.
3. Secure the mozzarella balls with toothpicks.
4. Preheat the air fryer to 360 F.
5. Put the mozzarella balls in the air fryer rack and cook for 10 minutes.

Nutrition: calories 262, fat 18.2, fiber 0.1, carbs 2.1, protein 22.1

Toasted Macadamia & Nuts Mix

Preparation time: 5 minutes

Cooking time: 9 minutes

Servings: 4

Ingredients:

- ¼ cup hazelnuts
- ¼ cup walnuts
- ½ cup pecans
- ½ cup macadamia nuts
- 1 tablespoon olive oil
- 1 teaspoon salt

Directions:

1. Preheat the air fryer to 320 F.
2. Place the hazelnuts, walnuts, pecans, and macadamia nuts in the air fryer.
3. Cook for 8 minutes stirring halfway through.
4. Drizzle the nuts with olive oil and salt and shake them well.
5. Cook the nuts for 1 minute.
6. Transfer the cooked nuts ramekins.

Nutrition: calories 230, fat 23.9, fiber 2.4, carbs 3.9, protein 3.9

Flax Mozzarella Wraps

Preparation time: 10 minutes

Cooking time: 2 minutes

Servings: 2

Ingredients:

- 1 cucumber
- 1 egg
- 3 oz. flax seeds
- 3 oz. mozzarella, grated
- 1 tablespoon water
- ½ tablespoon butter
- ¼ teaspoon baking soda
- ¼ teaspoon salt

Directions:

1. Crack the egg into a bowl and whisk it.
2. Sprinkle the whisked egg with the flax seeds, grated mozzarella, water, baking soda, and salt.
3. Whisk the mixture.
4. Preheat the air fryer to 360 F.
5. Toss the butter in the air fryer basket and melt it.
6. Separate the egg liquid into 2 servings.
7. Pour the first part of the serving in the air fryer basket.
8. Cook it for 1 minute on one side.
9. Turn over and cook for another minute.
10. Repeat the same steps with the remaining egg mixture.
11. Cut the cucumber into cubes.
12. Separate the cubed cucumber into 2 parts.
13. Place the cucumber cubes in the center of each egg pancake.
14. Wrap the eggs.

Nutrition: calories 143, fat 8.4, fiber 6.2, carbs 7.3, protein 8.6

Zucchini Fritters with Cheddar

Preparation time: 10 minutes

Cooking time: 8 minutes

Servings: 7

Ingredients:

- 4 oz. Mozzarella

- 3 oz. Cheddar cheese

- 1 zucchini, grated

- 2 tablespoon dried dill

- 1 tablespoon coconut flour

- 1 tablespoon almond flour

- ¼ teaspoon salt

- 1 teaspoon butter

Directions:

1. Shred the Cheddar and Mozzarella.
2. Combine the grated zucchini with the shredded cheese.
3. Add dried dill and coconut flour.
4. Add almond flour and salt.
5. Stir carefully with a fork.
6. Mix well to combine and leave to marinade for 3 minutes.
7. Preheat the air fryer to 400 F.
8. Melt the butter in the air fryer tray.
9. Make the fritters from the zucchini mixture and put them in the melted butter.
10. Cook the fritters for 5 minutes.
11. Turn the zucchini fritters over and cook for 3 minutes more.

Nutrition: calories 133, fat 9.6, fiber 1.3, carbs 3.7, protein 9.1

Keto Almond Buns

Preparation time: 15 minutes

Cooking time: 13 minutes

Servings: 10

Ingredients:

- 1 cup almond flour
- 5 tablespoon sesame seeds
- 1 tablespoon pumpkin seeds, crushed
- 1 teaspoon stevia extract
- ½ tablespoon baking powder
- 1 teaspoon apple cider vinegar
- ¼ teaspoon salt
- ½ cup water, hot
- 4 eggs

Directions:

1. Place the almond flour, sesame seeds, crushed pumpkin seeds, baking powder, and salt in a large mixing bowl.
2. Then crack the eggs in a separate bowl.
3. Whisk them and add stevia extract and apple cider vinegar.
4. Stir the egg mixture gently.
5. Pour the hot water into the almond flour mixture.
6. Stir and add the whisked egg mixture.
7. Knead the dough until well combined.
8. Preheat the air fryer to 350 F.
9. Cover the air fryer basket with some parchment paper.
10. Make 10 small buns from the dough and put them in the air fryer.
11. Cook the sesame cloud buns for 13 minutes.

12. Check if the buns are cooked. If they require a little more time – cook for 1 minute more.
13. Allow to cool before serving.

Nutrition: calories 72, fat 5.8, fiber 0.9, carbs 2.3, protein 3.8

DESSERT

Coconut Muffins

Preparation Time: 5 minutes

Cooking time: 25 minutes

Servings: 5

Ingredients:

- ½ cup coconut flour
- 2 tablespoons cocoa powder
- 3 tablespoons Erythritol
- 1 teaspoon baking powder
- 2 tablespoons coconut oil
- 2 eggs, beaten
- ½ cup coconut shred

Directions:

1. In the mixing bowl, mix all ingredients.
2. Then pour the mixture in the molds of the muffin and transfer in the air fryer basket.
3. Cook the muffins at 350F for 25 minutes.

Nutrition: calories 206, fat 16.7, fiber 7.1, carbs 13, protein 4.2

Coffee Muffins

Preparation time: 10 minutes

Cooking time: 11 minutes

Servings: 6

Ingredients:

- 1 cup coconut flour
- 4 tablespoons coconut oil
- 1 teaspoon vanilla extract
- 1 teaspoon instant coffee
- 1 teaspoon baking powder
- 1 egg, beaten
- ¼ cup Erythritol

Directions:

1. Mix coconut flour with coconut oil, vanilla extract, instant coffee, baking powder, egg, and Erythritol.

2. Put the mixture in the muffin molds and cook in the air fryer at 375F for 11 minutes.

Nutrition: calories 172, fat 11.8, fiber 8, carbs 13.9, protein 3.6

Almond Cookies

Preparation Time: 5 minutes

Cooking time: 15 minutes

Servings: 8

Ingredients:

- 1 cup almond flour

- 2 oz almonds, grinded

- 2 tablespoons Erythritol

- ½ teaspoon baking powder

- 5 tablespoons coconut oil, softened

- ½ teaspoon vanilla extract

Directions:

1. Mix almond flour with almonds, Erythritol, baking powder, coconut oil, and vanilla extract. Knead the dough.

2. Make the small cookies and place them in the air fryer basket.

3. Cook the cookies at 350F for 15 minutes.

Nutrition: calories 199, fat 18.7, fiber 2.4, carbs 4.7, protein 4.5

Thumbprint Cookies

Preparation time: 15 minutes

Cooking time: 9 minutes

Servings: 6

Ingredients:

- 2 teaspoons coconut oil, softened
- 1 tablespoon Erythritol
- 1 egg, beaten
- ½ cup coconut flour
- 1 oz almonds, chopped

Directions:

1. Mix all ingredients in the mixing bowl. Knead the dough.

2. Then make cookies from the dough and put in the air fryer basket.

3. Cook the cookies at 365F for 9 minutes.

Nutrition: calories 91, fat 5.6, fiber 4.6, carbs 10.2, protein 3.3

Pecan Bars

Preparation Time: 5 minutes

Cooking time: 40 minutes

Servings: 12

Ingredients:

- 2 cups coconut flour
- 5 tablespoons Erythritol
- 4 tablespoons coconut oil, softened
- ½ cup heavy cream
- 1 egg, beaten
- 4 pecans, chopped

Directions:

1. Mix coconut flour, Erythritol, coconut oil, heavy cream, and egg.
2. Pour the batter in the air fryer basket and flatten well.
3. Top the mixture with pecans and cook the meal at 350F for 40 minutes.
4. Cut the cooked meal into the bars.

Nutrition: calories 174, fat 12.1, fiber 8.5, carbs 14.2, protein 3.7

Brown Muffins

Preparation time: 15 minutes

Cooking time: 10 minutes

Servings: 2

Ingredients:

- 1 egg, beaten
- 1 tablespoon coconut oil, softened
- 2 tablespoons almond flour
- 1 tablespoon cocoa powder
- 1 tablespoon Erythritol
- 1 teaspoon ground cinnamon

Directions:

1. Mix egg with coconut oil, almond flour, cocoa powder, Erythritol, and ground cinnamon.

2. Pour the muffin batter in the muffin molds.

3. Bake the muffins at 375F for 10 minutes.

Nutrition: calories 141, fat 12.7, fiber 2.2, carbs 4.1, protein 4.8

Lime Bars

Preparation Time: 10 minutes

Cooking time: 35 minutes

Servings: 10

Ingredients:

- 3 tablespoons coconut oil, melted
- 3 tablespoons Splenda
- 1 ½ cup coconut flour
- 3 eggs, beaten
- 1 teaspoon lime zest, grated
- 3 tablespoons lime juice

Directions:

1. Cover the air fryer basket bottom with baking paper.
2. Then in the mixing bowl, mix Splenda with coconut flour, eggs, lime zest, and lime juice.
3. Pour the mixture in the air fryer basket and flatten gently.
4. Cook the meal at 350F for 35 minutes.
5. Then cool the cooked meal little and cut into bars.

Nutrition: calories 144, fat 7.2, fiber 7.2, carbs 15.7, protein 4.1

Tender Macadamia Bars

Preparation time: 15 minutes

Cooking time: 30 minutes

Servings: 10

Ingredients:

- 3 tablespoons butter, softened
- 1 teaspoon baking powder
- 1 teaspoon apple cider vinegar
- 1.5 cup coconut flour
- 3 tablespoons swerve
- 1 teaspoon vanilla extract
- 2 eggs, beaten
- 2 oz macadamia nuts, chopped
- Cooking spray

Directions:

1. Spray the air fryer basket with cooking spray.

2. Then mix all remaining ingredients in the mixing bowl and stir until you get a homogenous mixture.

3. Pour the mixture in the air fryer basket and cook at 345F for 30 minutes.

4. When the mixture is cooked, cut it into bars and transfer in the serving plates.

Nutrition: calories 158, fat 10.4, fiber 7.7, carbs 13.1, protein 4

Cinnamon Zucchini Bread

Preparation Time: 10 minutes

Cooking time: 40 minutes

Servings: 12

Ingredients:

- 2 cups coconut flour
- 2 teaspoons baking powder
- ¾ cup Erythritol
- ½ cup coconut oil, melted
- 1 teaspoon apple cider vinegar
- 1 teaspoon vanilla extract
- 3 eggs, beaten
- 1 zucchini, grated
- 1 teaspoon ground cinnamon

Directions:

1. In the mixing bowl, mix coconut flour with baking powder, Erythritol, coconut oil, apple cider vinegar, vanilla extract, eggs, zucchini, and ground cinnamon.

2. Transfer the mixture in the air fryer basket and flatten it in the shape of the bread.

3. Cook the bread at 350F for 40 minutes.

Nutrition: calories 179, fat 12.2, fiber 8.3, carbs 14.6, protein 4.3

Poppy Seeds Muffins

Preparation time: 10 minutes

Cooking time: 10 minutes

Servings: 5

Ingredients:

- 5 tablespoons coconut oil, softened
- 1 egg, beaten
- 1 teaspoon vanilla extract
- 1 tablespoon poppy seeds
- 1 teaspoon baking powder
- 2 tablespoons Erythritol
- 1 cup coconut flour

Directions:

1. In the mixing bowl, mix coconut oil with egg, vanilla extract, poppy seeds, baking powder, Erythritol, and coconut flour.

2. When the mixture is homogenous, pour it in the muffin molds and transfer it in the air fryer basket.

3. Cook the muffins for 10 minutes at 365F.

Nutrition: calories 239, fat 17.7, fiber 9.8, carbs 17.1, protein 4

CONCLUSION

Living the keto lifestyle can be tough, but only if you allow it to be.

Counting your carbohydrates

Measuring your carb intake is extremely important and should never be neglected. Being lackadaisical about doing this in time will become a part of your routine, and that would eventually defeat the aim of the dieting. So, in order to prevent this, you need to constantly read the labels on foods you're having and ensure that the carbohydrates proportions are suitable for your daily allowance. Whenever you are out in a grocery store, ensure you read the labels on everything you purchase. Undeniably, it may be burdensome, but it will be worth it in the end. When deciding the carb count in foods, calculate the net carbs (net carbs = total carbs – fiber).

Your goal should be to consume about 20 net carbs per day. It is perfectly alright if there are substitutes, but the rule is to consume an intake of 20 to 35 net carbs a day. But if you are exercising, it is advisable that you eat your daily net carbs before you begin exercising as your body will burn glucose during the exercise and revert to using ketones subsequently. Having a small carb intake before exercising is an excellent idea to acquiring some quick energy into your body so that you can take your workout all the way.

Make sure that during your first months, you maintain a record of what you are consuming daily. Sometimes it can be a mere blunder or a snack that drives you over the carb threshold.

Clean out your kitchen

Many people fall to the temptation of food quite easily. Do your best not to be one of them. Do away with any food that is high in carbohydrates in your kitchen or refrigerator; this is especially the case in candies, chocolates, caffeine, sodas, juices, bread, gluten, pasta, rice, potatoes, etc. If you don't want to throw away all these foods, simply give it to a friend, family member, neighbor, or donate.

After that, head to the grocery store, execute your new label reading tactics and renew your fridge and pantry with low-carb options to feed on. Believe me; you will feel better about this once your food addictions are conquered

Keto diets and restaurants

When you begin a keto-friendly lifestyle, be mindful of what kind of diners and restaurants you are going to. You may want to go over an online menu in advance, so you know exactly what you'll get and have the carb count. In due course, you can order from menus in restaurants you have never gone in before as you can calculate the net carbs in every recipe. Below are some ketogenic-friendly orders you can find in almost all restaurants:

For breakfast: eggs, bacon, and sausage.

For lunch: chicken salad (without salad dressings)

For dinner: meat!

Eating low carb actively

Fast foods, snacks, and cravings will always be present in our lives. Be sure to have your refrigerator and pantry stored with snacks to eat if you're in a rush or starving. If you have works to do, ensure you pack your lunch in advance along with a snack.

Now, strict adherence to these steps will assure you of a higher chance of attaining a successful ketogenic diet journey!

30 DAYS MEAL PLAN

Day	Breakfast	Snacks	Dinner
1	Mozzarella Tots	Parsley Shrimp Tails	Lettuce Salad with Beef Strips
2	Chicken Balls	Calamari Almond Rings	Cayenne Rib Eye Steak
3	Tofu Egg Scramble	Keto Beef Bombs	Beef-Chicken Meatball Casserole
4	Flax & Hemp Porridge	Paprika Mozzarella Balls	Juicy Pork Chops
5	Creamy Bacon Eggs	Toasted Macadamia & Nuts Mix	Chicken Goulash
6	Cheddar Bacon Hash	Flax Mozzarella Wraps	Chicken & Turkey Meatloaf
7	Cheddar Soufflé with Herbs	Zucchini Fritters with Cheddar	Turkey Meatballs with Dried Dill
8	Bacon Butter Biscuits	Keto Almond Buns	Parmesan Beef Slices
9	Keto Parmesan Frittata	Avocado in Bacon Wraps	Chili Beef Jerky
10	Chicken Liver Pate	Herbed Crab Cakes	Spinach Beef Heart
11	Coconut Pancake Hash	Jalapeno Bacon Bites	Chicken Coconut Poppers
12	Beef Slices	Chicken Nuggets	Chicken Goulash
13	Cheddar Bacon Hash	Moroccan Lamb Balls	Paprika Pulled Pork
14	Egg Clouds	Flax Mozzarella Wraps	Paprika Whole Chicken
15	Flax & Chia Porridge	Onion Circles	Pork Almond Bites
16	Parmesan Ham Hash	Scotch Beef Eggs	Pandan Coconut Chicken

17	Paprika Eggs with Bacon	Turmeric Eggplants	Bacon Chicken Breast
18	Eggs in Avocado	Creamy Cauliflower Florets	Cheddar Chicken Drumsticks
19	Baked Cheddar Egg Cups	Zucchini Egg Fritters	Garlic Beef Steak
20	Cauliflower Fritters	Chili Chicken Bites	Coriander Chicken
21	Egg-Beef Rolls	Tomato Beef Meatballs	Air Frier Pork Ribs
22	Paprika Egg Rolls	Oregano Chicken Wings	Paprika Beef Tongue
23	Chicken-Pork Sausages	Keto French Fries	Almond Salmon Pie
24	Almond Blackberry Muffins	Paprika Zucchini Chips	Garlic Beef Mash
25	Parmesan Ham Hash	Radish Chips	Corn Chive Beef
26	Beef Cheddar Chili	Paprika Avocado Fries	Pepper Beef Stew
27	Cheddar Chicken Casserole	Eggplant Bites with Parmesan	Garlic Chicken Curry
28	Paprika Eggs	Creamy Cauliflower Florets	Thyme Shredded Beef
29	Crunchy Canadian Bacon	Ginger Chicken Wings	Beef Strips with Zucchini Zoodles
30	Kale Fritters	Lamb Chives Burgers	Garlic Beef Mash

CPSIA information can be obtained
at www.ICGtesting.com
Printed in the USA
LVHW051130110621
689903LV00004B/393